Distributed by
DUNELLEN PUBLISHING COMPANY, INC.
145 East 52nd Street, New York, New York 10022

New Trends in Kremlin Policy

The Center for
Strategic and International Studies
Georgetown University
Washington, D. C.
Special Report Series: No. 11
August 1970

The Center for Strategic and International
Studies' *Special Reports* offer the specialist and
the general reader a series of topical analyses of
international issues. Each report is prepared by
an interdisciplinary panel, which defines the
scope of the study and guides the staff work.
Panel findings and recommendations are issued
with each report and these are supplemented
with comments from individual panelists in
order to preserve their diverse views.

Foreword

For the Soviet leadership, 1970 is a year of multiple, interrelated, complex and crucial decisions. A new Party Congress long overdue has now been summoned to meet in the Kremlin in March 1971. The repeated postponements of the Congress, in violation of Party Statutes, may be one indication of the depth and intensity of the conflicts within Soviet policy and within the leadership. Important changes in leadership have customarily been carried out in advance of a congress, which then ratifies and acclaims them. Will that hold true in 1970-1971?

A new Five-year Plan, for 1971-1975, is being prepared, and there is clear evidence of deepset struggles over the future course to be set for the economy. An issue, unresolved and basically unresolvable, which festers on and on, is whether and how far to tolerate mild dissent and cautious experimentation; the conflict continues to plague the ruling Party in its relations with the upper ranks of planners, managers, scientists, writers, and artists.

As the leadership looks to its problems in the outer world, it faces simultaneously a whole range of dilemmas. What attitudes should it adopt toward the massive hostility of China? Toward the strategic and political competition with the United States? Toward the beclouded prospects in South East Asia? And especially toward the expanding opportunities and risks that confront Soviet ambitions in the Middle East?

When Nikita Khrushchev launched the Soviet Union in 1955 on an active and versatile campaign to achieve preponderant influence in the Arab world, he could hardly have envisaged the many gains that Soviet policy has won since then, or the rising level of risks and costs that the logic of ever-deepening involvement has brought with it. Should the Kremlin seek now to stabilize its gains, or should it press its present and precarious advantages ever closer to possible great-power showdown? Can the Kremlin henceforth control the level of its risks in exploiting the Arab-Israeli conflict without jeopardizing its political alliance with various groups and shadings of Arab nationalism? Will an all-out attempt to expel U.S. and western influences once and for all from the Eastern Mediterranean revitalize the western nations' sense of danger? Or will it promote a wave of disintegration in the Atlantic alliance?

Will a future China without Mao maintain flinchingly its massive defiance of Soviet economic and military might and its challenge to Soviet ideological primacy? With Mao gone, will it sooner or later seek a new accommodation with the Soviet state? Or will it turn to one of several varieties of "peaceful co-existence" with noncommunist nations?

Will the weakening of U.S. efforts and influence in Viet Nam promote a new intensification of Sino-Soviet competition? Or will the emerging situation in South East Asia lead Moscow and Peking to seek a division of roles, or even of spheres of pre-dominant influence in Asia?

Should the Kremlin attempt to establish a more stable rela-tionship with the United States? Is "parity" an end in itself or only a stage? Since the Soviet Union now has a "sufficiency" of nuclear power, should it seek in the 1970s to stabilize the nuclear equation and to restrain the ballooning costs of nuclear escala-tion? Can a meaningful and stable "parity" between the two great nuclear powers be defined in terms of a relatively reliable system of arms control? Or is the Soviet Union seeking to achieve a numerical "superiority" over U.S. nuclear power, in order to impress both allies and enemies by an outward display of "suprem-acy" over U.S. strategic might? Presenting the world with a clear-cut superiority in numbers of nuclear weapons may appear to some leaders in the Kremlin a feasible political means for consolidating its own alliances and disintegrating the opposing forces. Such a major shift in the worldwide balance of power may also heighten the risks of confrontation, with vast costs in the present and unfore-seeable dangers in the future.

The Soviet invasion of "fraternal" Czechoslovakia in 1968 won the Kremlin a respite in its search for solutions to its dilemma there; it has not provided any permanent solutions. The question of accommodating Soviet demands for ideological conformity and political subservience to the national interests and nationalist emotions of communist-ruled satellites remains unresolved. The problem of whose interests are to be respected and which are to be sacrificed will plague Kremlin policy makers throughout the 1970s.

Can the Soviet economy sustain the rising costs of maintaining a tightened control over the satellite economies without slowing down its own rate of growth? Can the Soviet Union afford indefinitely the political costs of reenforcing the economic integration of the Soviet bloc and simultaneously pursuing a policy of shifting onto its satellites the increasing costs of forced integration? Can the imposition of ideological conformity on the dependent nations of Eastern Europe avoid the pitfall of stagnation and apathy without some day opening the door to the pent-up pressures of national self-assertion?

The forthcoming economic decisions at home, in the Soviet Union, are closely connected with the dilemmas of Soviet policy beyond its borders. Despite many lags and deficiencies, the Soviet economy is both powerful and growing. Yet, its dynamic rate of growth has slackened markedly in recent years. Will the Kremlin do more in the next half decade than in the past to make industry more productive, modernize a largely archaic agriculture, and provide the more adequate incentives that are needed to stimulate a higher level of productivity? Can it do more in these fields, so essential to an increasingly complex economy and to a greater satisfaction of domestic needs? And can it at the same time pour vast resources into the spiralling budgets of nuclear competition, into military and economic largesse to allies and potential allies, and into a long-range plan to acquire influence (and costly responsibilities) in a number of underdeveloped regions of the world? The hammering out of a system of national priorities has provoked debates and indecision within the Soviet leadership, and this in turn complicates and slows down the processes of decision making.

Finally, the Kremlin faces in the 1970s the problem of renewing its top cadres and modernizing its methods of control and leadership. Decades of promises unfulfilled have accumulated a massive apathy among workers and collective-farm peasants, among the youth, which sees the future as a continuation of a drab present, among the non-Russian nationalities, and among the creative part of the intelligentsia, which, while small in numbers, makes vital contributions to the processes of scientific, intellectual, economic, and technological progress. In its response, the Soviet leadership has repeatedly shifted the uneasy balance between slackening and tightening the reins. Clearly, important decisions in this crucial area of policy cannot be avoided, and the pressures for new decisions coincide in time with inevitable changes in the top leadership and its style of rule.

Postponed and unavoidable decisions await action. The 1970s may well mark a new turning-point in many crucial aspects of Soviet policy. Hence, any additional light that can be thrown into the dark corners of Kremlin thinking and motives can be very helpful to the western world in clarifying its understanding of the prospects of Kremlin policy. It is in response to this need that the Center for Strategic and International Studies of Georgetown University undertook the study presented here. First, it invited a wide range of experienced and perceptive analysts to prepare brief and pointed projections of Soviet policy in the 1970s. It then invited two panels, one in the United States and one in Europe, to take part in an intensive debate on the prospects for Soviet action. The Center now presents to a wider public the results, in succinct form, of this systematic effort to examine the basic factors and problems that will shape the new trends of Soviet policy in the 1970s.

PHILIP E. MOSELY
Chairman
Research Council

Table of Contents

Foreword v

Part One: Panel Findings
Preface 3

I. European Panel Findings 7
Economic Problems; Leadership Struggles at the Top; Influence of Military Power; Strategic Military Balance; Anti-Ballistic Missiles; National Interests v. Ideology in Foreign Policy; Prospects for Negotiations with West; Relations with Eastern Europe; Relations with China; 1969 World Conference of Communist Parties.

II. American Panel Findings 23
Economic problems; Leadership Struggles at the Top; National Interests v. Ideology in Foreign Policy; Restalinization: Characteristics and Effects; Relations with Eastern Europe; Relations with China.

Part Two: The Background Paper
I. Introduction 36
II. The Final Years of the Khrushchev Decade 39
III. The Rise of the Soviet Military-Industrial Apparatus Complex 45
IV. Changing Modes of Destalinization 59
V. The Stalin Issue in Perspective 63
VI. Why Restalinization? 70
VII. The Contemporary Crisis in Foreign Policy 81
VIII. New Departures in Foreign Policy 85
IX. The Sino-Soviet Controversy 95
X. The Triangulation of Global Power 103
XI. The Temptations and Risks of Strategic Superiority 107
XII. Eastern Europe Since Czechoslovakia 115
XIII. Soviet Policy Aims in Eastern Europe 119
XIV. Soviet Control Tightened in Eastern Europe 122
XV. The Results of Soviet Efforts 126
XVI. Some Specific Cases 131
XVII. Prospects in Eastern Europe 144

Part Three: Individual Panelist Comments
I. European Panelists 149
Sir William Hayter, Professor Alec Nove, Ambassador Gebhardt von Walther, Dr. Gehard Wettig

II. American Panelists 153
Mr. Abraham Brumberg, Dr. Richard Burks, Amb. Foy Kohler, Dr. Wolfgang Leonhard, Dr. Kurt London

PART ONE

Panel Findings

Preface

The relevance of this study to U.S. foreign policy has been enhanced by President Nixon's special message to Congress on February 18 entitled "U.S. Foreign Policy for the 1970's: A New Strategy for Peace." In that message the President declared: "The central problem of Soviet-American relations . . . is whether our two countries can transcend the past and work together to build a lasting peace."

This report addresses some of the principal developments of recent history in Soviet domestic affairs, foreign policy, and relationships with Eastern Europe bearing on this problem. Its primary purpose is to provide background and analysis of forces and trends that may play a major role in assessing future courses of U.S. foreign policy on matters that are greatly influenced by Soviet intentions.

Hopefully this report will shed light on such matters as: 1) The relevance of earlier Soviet perceptions concerning purposes of the state to the era we are now entering; 2) The extent to which Soviet leadership reflects changing views of ideology's role in policy; 3) The extent to which leadership is prepared to approach international problems on a pragmatic basis, with a willingness to seek realistic accommodations of conflicting interests; 4) The nature and stability of the Soviet decision-making process, especially the struggles for leadership within the Soviet Union and the influence of the Soviet military; 5) Problems of the Soviet economy, prospects of reform, and the capabilities of the economy to continue high levels of military expenditure; 6) Implications of the changing strategic military balance and the Soviet views of the anti-ballistic missile problem; 7) The likelihood of sustained Soviet pursuit of global political goals and the degree of risk of the use of force by the U.S.S.R. in their pursuit; 8) The extent to which Soviet leaders realize the need for preventing small crises from escalating into major ones and what the United States can do to influence this process; 9) Prospects that a gradual, practical process of agreement building between the U.S.S.R. and other states will lead to a lasting peace; 10) The evolution of forces within Eastern Europe and the impact of change in that area on the Soviet Union; 11) The significance of the Sino-Soviet dispute in Soviet assessments of policy alternatives.

Since the preparation of this report, which spanned the past year and a half, there have been several developments in related areas that go beyond the scope of our analysis. For example, the Soviet Union has made increasing progress in the deployment of strategic offensive weapons systems. This leads to a forecast of some Soviet superiority in this critical area of weapons development. Contemplation of this change in the military balance raises important questions about Soviet willingness to risk direct intervention and confrontation with the United States particularly in the Third World. The Soviet leadership might attempt to translate changes in the correlation of military forces into new political initiatives. Alternatively, forces may be at work—perhaps resulting from shifts in top Soviet leadership or unanticipated difficulties in Soviet economic growth—that may contribute to continued restraint or to a new willingness to pursue unexplored avenues of détente.

Another interesting aspect of internal Soviet development that may cause concern is the possibility that at the present time Soviet leadership may be growing weaker in relation to the increasing strength of Soviet military power. This combination is always a dangerous one because of the tendencies on the part of such regimes to compensate for internal inefficiencies by external activism.

Subsequent research by The Center for Strategic and International Studies on the Indian Ocean, Africa, Latin America, and the Western Pacific will address to a greater extent Soviet policies in and towards the under-developed areas. Previous Center publications, e.g., *Soviet Seapower* and *NATO after Czechoslovakia*, have addressed interactions of Soviet policy in other regions.

The Center deeply appreciates the contributions made to the conclusions of this report by the many eminent panelists whose names are listed elsewhere. Special thanks are owed to Professor Laurence Martin of the University of London, a member of the Center's Research Council, for his skillful moderation of the discussions of the European panel held in Brussels on May 26, 1969. The Center also wishes to acknowledge the outstanding research by the primary authors of the background paper: Dr. Vernon V. Aspaturian, Director of the Slavic and Soviet Language and Area Center, Pennsylvania State University; and Dr. James F. Brown, formerly of Columbia University, now with Radio Free Europe. Noteworthy additions on the Sino-Soviet controversy were received from Dr. Jay Sorenson, Professor of Political Science, University of New Mexico, and on the Soviet economy from Dr. John Hardt of Research Analysis Corporation. Other contributions to the background papers were made by members of the Center staff. The synthesis of the panel findings for the European Panel, updating and collation of the background papers was performed by the undersigned. The findings of the U.S. Panel were summarized by Byron Hallsted of George Washington University. The editing of this study was done by Richard Whalen, writer-in-residence at the Center. Special mention should be made of the fine work done by Dr. Alvin Cottrell, Research Director of the Center, in organizing and directing the early phases of the project. Also, we are indebted to Dr. Lincoln Landis of the Battelle Memorial Institute for help in getting the project initiated. Appreciative mention should also be made of the research assistance provided by Ethel Eanet and by Anne Garber of the Center staff.

ROBERT A. KILMARX
Project Director

European
Panel
Findings

There is at present no sense of economic crisis among the Soviet leadership, which appears to consider that resources can be used more efficiently solely by making relatively minor improvements in traditional methods.

Declining capital productivity was a matter of great concern when the new collective leadership assumed power in 1965, but subsequent economic progress dispersed the fear of serious industrial deceleration and with it the sense of urgency in the apparent need for sweeping reorganization. Limited reforms have probably eased economic strains, which have, in any case, not induced any reduction in military appropriations or other calls on the economy in pursuit of foreign policy objectives.

The forces of inertia and conservatism in the political and economic administration have combined with these developments to severely limit reforms. The economic strains that persist result in inevitable conflicts between various policy priorities. There is a commitment to improving living standards and housing, and substantial resources are being devoted to agriculture. In Russia, as elsewhere, the demands of the military do run up against budgetary constraints. Foreign aid is unpopular and the government knows it. Nevertheless, the present level of military appropriations and of aid can be sustained without undue economic strain and military spending can increase with rising national income.

The real resources devoted to the military production sector of the economy in the U.S.S.R. in comparison with the United States are much higher than the relative proportions of the GNP would suggest, for costs are lower and efficiency higher than in other sectors. Despite the lack of firm evidence, it has been maintained that the correct valuation of the Soviet ruble in this sector may be as high as 42 kopeks to the U.S. dollar, against an official exchange rate of 90 kopeks.

The major area of difficulty remains in agriculture. The reforms, as yet only beginning, may be characterized as a "withdrawal from arbitrariness." They have resulted in greater economic freedom for farmers, more stable quotas for delivery to state agencies, and higher prices. From a political point of view further reform along such lines would not be as challenging to the regime as any comparable industrial change.

Such reforms could encourage initiative among agricultural producers, while at the same time maintaining to a considerable degree the control of the State over procurements, i.e. over the supply of basic foodstuffs for towns, for the army, and for export. In the industrial sector, the devolution of authority to the enterprise manager could threaten the pattern of the political authority in the system. There is less scope for the introduction of market principles in the industrial sector without raising major political issues. The party is accustomed to exercising its control by direct administrative intervention over production and distribution in industry. In agriculture, its control is confined to procurements. Recent events in Czechoslovakia have strengthened opposition in principle to the very idea of market socialism. It is not clear whether this opposition is due to fear that market socialism would lead to political reform, or whether it is simply the conservative response of an establishment that is accustomed to the present system and benefits from it.

Leadership Struggles at the Top

A marked change appears to have occurred in top-level Soviet decision-making since Khrushchev. Once a major decision is reached, the present Soviet leadership seems to stick to it. While the composition of the preeminent group within the Politburo—apart from Brezhnev—may be uncertain to outside analysts, there appears to be a dominant *troika*—Brezhnev, Kosygin and Suslov. They seem to realize that unless they cling together, all are in danger. According to one view, as long as the three members move in unison, there is little serious danger to the structure as a whole. Unlike the situation under Khrushchev, the hazard of factions is reduced by the appearance of one or two members of the *troika* at at every Politburo meeting.

The *troika* is not powerful enough, however, to resolve all issues alone—particularly the less important ones affecting domestic affairs. The entire Politburo may be involved in such questions. The vulnerability of the *troika* to criticism was revealed after the 1967 Arab-Israeli War. Even when the *troika* and the full membership of the Politburo decide by majority vote, an issue may not be finally settled. Minority views may be raised again when the opportunity presents itself.

It seems unlikely that a small group like the *troika* can alter the course of the bureaucracy more effectively than in the past. As the Soviet economy becomes more complex, many decisions must be made at lower levels. The diffusion of decision-making, however, is primarily within the bureaucracy. Industrial managers have their impact on policy primarily through ministers and other members of the government drawn from their ranks.

Although disagreements over policy cannot be characterized as power struggles, public allusions to seemingly mild differences of opinion may reflect harsh political conflict. Harmony within the Politburo is an abnormal condition, for the men near the top in the Soviet system dare not trust each other. The struggle for power is inherent in the system, and it assumes forms unlike those in any other society.

Because all key decisions, even those of a technical nature, are ultimately political, and because decisions are made and leaders designated in secret, a condition of chronic instability results. As soon as disagreement is expressed in the Politburo, the members recognize that the issue of personal survival lurks in the background. The tendency toward conflict may be compounded by the efforts of an aging political leadership (averaging 59 years in the Central Committee) to exclude younger contenders. When this rising generation makes its breakthrough, however, it may be even more arrogant and chauvinistic than its predecessor.

The central issue in a particular power struggle varies as circumstances change. In the period 1953-57, the contenders for power had to lend support to the needs of the consumer. Now the central theme seems to be chauvinism, and contenders are bound to be super-patriotic. During the last few years, it has been evident that such competitive chauvinism can cause an escalation of foreign policy issues. The current climate within the Politburo can breed competition to strike aggressive postures toward the outside world. This could raise a greater danger of words leading to deeds of an explosive nature, although it is recognized that the present Soviet leaders have been cautious about undertaking dangerous foreign adventures.

Rival members of the leadership look for support from elements within the system enjoying a strong power base. These elements are primarily the K.G.B., the armed forces, the military industrial complex and the bureaucratic apparatus. The party apparatus may also be viewed as a potential power base. In their search for allies, rival power seekers must pay particular attention to the military.

Influence of litary Power Brezhnev, who appears to be a prime initiator of contemporary Soviet foreign policy, has forged strong ties with the military establishment. Within the Politburo, he is in charge of army interests. Although he would run grave risks of being overturned if he openly courted army support, his voice has special authority because of his special relationship to the military.

There is an important difference between a power-seeker's reliance on the secret police and on the army. The secret police is unpopular with the people, but it can find support for its views in the Politburo by appealing to fears of a threat to Soviet security. The army is popular with the people, but the Politburo is afraid of the army's popularity. Military influence goes up and down, but the degree of this influence has historically been restricted by an exaggerated fear of Bonapartism. The intense concern over Bonapartism limits the extent to which contenders for power can depend on Soviet military support in the struggle for survival. Still, it is an historical fact that when a crisis occurs—as in 1953, 1956, 1957, and 1964—the person who forfeits army support loses.

Strategic-Military Balance At the level of strategic offensive-defensive nuclear capabilities, both the U.S.S.R. and the United States have the means to maintain a valid second-strike capability in the foreseeable future. Neither side is generally believed to be in a position to obtain a valid first-strike capability. In fact, it is assumed that the Soviets have an incentive to keep the two sides near their present positions rather than undergo the cost of another round in the arms race. It is further assumed that a majority within the Politburo favors strategic arms limitation talks with the United States, realizing that the two sides have effectively neutralized each other at this level.

If this assumption should prove false and the

U.S.S.R. should be permitted to obtain some degree of first-strike capability, the Soviets would be in a position to pursue expansionist aims through threats. It is considered unlikely, however, that the U.S. would lack the will as well as the capability to block the U.S.S.R. from obtaining a meaningful first-strike capability. Nevertheless, lower levels of relative advantage are not meaningless in diplomacy, especially in a confrontation where the alternative, as seen by one side, is not between peace and conflict but between striking first or second.

In regard to the military balance in Europe for the predictable future, it is concluded that the Soviets would find inconvenient, if not objectionable, a unified Germany—even under a Communist administration. They might seek to block such a development but could not veto it. It is not inconceivable, however, that at some future date a different view might prevail, if a unified Germany were subservient to Moscow and effectively served the purposes of Soviet policy.

The U.S.S.R. is determined to maintain its strong presence in Eastern Europe, partly for military and partly for political reasons. From a military standpoint, it provides a glacis—an area for military deployment and thus a shield to Soviet territory. From a political standpoint, it provides backup for the maintenance of orthodoxy in Eastern Europe. Thus, little change in the overall strategic military balance in Europe is to be anticipated in the immediate future.

Regarding peacetime activity in distant overseas areas, Soviet leaders are believed to be prepared to probe and experiment with the objective of expansion. They probably see an advantage in putting as much effort as possible into this area of confrontation. The initial goal is to extend the Soviet presence through naval power. The longer-term goal may be to acquire the power to intervene in support of a pro-Soviet political movement or a favored side in a civil war. The west faces the prospect of a more active, competitive, and interventionist Soviet political and military policy on the global scale, notwithstanding that it will probably remain cautious about risks of military conflict with the United States.

Anti-Ballistic Missiles The Soviet press has placed extraordinary emphasis on discussions within the United States concerning the Anti-Ballistic Missile program, and has stressed the costs involved in such weapon systems. This is the first time Soviet leaders have given the people an accurate idea of the tremendous sums of money required for modern weapons.

There are several possible interpretations of this. A faction within the Soviet leadership may be seeking to stress the costs of ABM as part of its position in an ongoing arms debate about the desirability of such a weapon system. This interpretation would imply that no final decision has been made concerning major expenditures in this crucial area. On the other hand, these articles may be primarily designed to convince the noncommunist world that it is leading an excessively costly arms race by proceeding with ABM deployment. Or the purpose of these articles may be to persuade the Soviet people of the necessity for a continued slowdown in consumer spending and further cutbacks in the nonmilitary sector of the economy in order to meet new defense requirements. The last interpretation is supported by Kosygin's statements on the need to give high priority to defense spending because the arms race is being conducted by the noncommunist powers. The Russian people generally support without complaint expenditures for armaments, especially for defense.

National Interests v. Ideology in Foreign Policy Since the founding of the Soviet regime, the noncommunist world has tried to determine the relative importance of state and ideological interests in the U.S.S.R.'s foreign policy. This distinction is meaningful only where a conflict results from the pursuit of one set of interests and values as opposed to another. A dichotomy of state and party interests, however, is institutionalized in the Communist Party of the Soviet Union and governmental apparatus. Inevitably, ideology will make itself felt in policy, but the question remains: to what extent? For example, the Soviet motive in invading Czechoslovakia was clearly security. It does not matter greatly how security considerations were weighed between military and ideological factors. In the case of Vietnam, it may be true that ideological interests have been more significant than state interests, but state interests now may equally impel the continuation of a war that has very adverse results for the United States.

Even the Soviet leaders themselves probably cannot draw a neat distinction between state and ideological interests. They would maintain that any attempt to draw such a distinction would be absurd. Soviet leaders make policy on the basis of state interests, which rest on ideological premises. State interests are shaped by the perceptions of ideology. While ideology is, in part, little more than a card index of quotations useful to the Soviet leadership to justify actions taken on other grounds, it is also a way of looking at and distorting reality. The fundamental confrontation with capitalistic countries, for example, is a self-evident and enduring truth. Residual Soviet ideological fervor in the form of self-righteousness—the belief that the Soviets alone possess final truth and can provide the only source of virtue—results in further distortion. The Soviets continue to look at a world divided by struggle.

We must conclude, however, that the impact of ideology on foreign policy varies somewhat at different levels of policy formulation in the U.S.S.R. Soviet foreign policy can be broken down into policies toward other communist parties, toward the Third World and toward the capitalistic countries. Policy toward the

Third World and toward capitalistic countries may be viewed as more "normal" or traditional foreign relations, though still affected by ideological goals; policy toward other communist parties are more greatly influenced by ideology.

Two of the key factors which determine the impact of ideology on state interests are rapidly advancing technology and the changing strategic military balances. Both in noncommunist and in communist circles, these cause re-evaluation of long accepted premises and positions.

Prospects for
negotiations
with West

Recently, Soviet internal policy indicates efforts are again being made to rebuild the Iron Curtain. This trend raises the question: Is a tightened Soviet internal policy compatible with a 'détente policy' toward the noncommunist governments? As the Soviets enter arms control negotiations, such internal conditions cast shadows of doubt as to their intentions.

It can be argued that no contradiction exists. This conclusion can be supported by historical evidence. For example, during the period of Litvinov, Soviet disarmament overtures coincided with severe internal repressions. It may also be argued that if the Soviets feel compelled to seek an accommodation with the United States in strategic weapons, they may judge it necessary to tighten up internally and thus avoid pressures for a domestic counterpart of a more relaxed foreign policy.

The situation poses a dilemma for the noncommunist nations rather than for the Soviet Union. As long as the United States is willing to talk with the U.S.S.R., regardless of internal repressions, the Soviets are free to continue divergent policies without adverse consequences.

The panel could not reach a consensus on prospects of negotiations with the Soviets.

Some panelists conclude that the Russians would never be able to talk on a fundamental basis with the Americans because of ideological hostility. Although occasional, limited negotiations might succeed, no full-scale agreement to settle world problems could be anticipated. Even if the Russians should desire basic agreements, some panelists believe that they are too distrustful to be able to make them.

Other panelists take a different view. They conclude that there is a fundamental change in style in Soviet leadership. Negotiations are now possible, with give and take and even some measure of trust. Clouds of ideological verbiage are put up when the Russians do not want to make agreements, yet they can talk sense and control their suspicions when they want to settle something for the sake of expediency.

Others on the panel, seeking to bridge the opposing judgments, see some circumstances where the Soviets and Americans can reach agreements on matters involving "unwanted crises." The Russians are believed to be prepared to develop techniques for negotiating with the Americans on specific issues. Nevertheless, it seems unlikely to these panelists that rapprochement can be achieved. The Soviets need a degree of ideological tension for internal reasons. Otherwise, it is impossible to explain the sacrifices imposed on the population.

Relations with Eastern Europe Soviet relations with Eastern Europe are based on four fundamental requirements that are imposed on the states in the area:

> *One,* the region must continue to provide a political as well as military glacis for Soviet security.
>
> *Two,* orthodox communist regimes must be maintained in Eastern Europe, with each state ruled by a government that is obedient to the norms laid down by Moscow. Certain internal reforms may

be adopted in the interest of economic efficiency, but not at the expense of political orthodoxy as defined by the Soviet Union.

Three, Eastern European countries must accept Soviet evaluations of events and trends, not only in Eastern Europe, but within the global communist movement and the world at large. The Soviet view of military and subversive threats from the outside is the only acceptable view at the present time.

Four, Eastern Europeans should falsify their own history and national identity, as required, to correspond with the changing needs of Soviet policy.

There are five basic anomalies, however, between what the Soviets want and what they can attain. These contradictions prevent their requirements from being fulfilled as the Soviets would wish.

One, the Soviets find it increasingly difficult to cope with forces of nationalism. Eastern European states continually attempt to decide for themselves what their national interests are.

Two, Soviet policies toward West Germany are fashioned in its own interest and without much regard to East Germany's wishes, especially if those wishes do not coincide with Moscow's intentions. The East German regime, however, remains unconditionally loyal to the U.S.S.R., as it perceives no future for itself outside the closest cooperation with the Soviet Union. The interests of East Germany can be viewed as more important to the whole "camp" than those of other states in that area.

Three, the younger generation increasingly questions the requirements laid down from Moscow.

Four, in each country the drive for economic efficiency poses problems for the Soviet Union—for example, in The Council for Mutual Economic Assistance (COMECON). Some Eastern European states, i.e. Czechoslovakia, Hungary and tentatively, Bulgaria, regard COMECON as a means toward creation of a free trade area (such as The European Free Trade Area, E.F.T.A.), in which nationalized enterprises or public corporations can compete among members of the group within guidelines from each government. The fiscal and tariff system would not be unlike that of a market economy. Rumania, which has been the last of the group to reorganize its directive mechanism, also supports change. Only in Hungary is reform being pursued as it was conceived before the Czechoslovak crisis. The Soviet position is for close economic integration along strictly intergovernmental lines. Yet the need for economic reform in Eastern Europe remains more urgent than in the U.S.S.R.

Five, unable to believe that a regime dependent on public opinion and popular support will remain reliable politically and militarily, the Soviet leaders cannot accept the prospect of Czech-type "democratic" socialism in Eastern Europe.

The Soviets do not accept these contradictions as obstacles to carrying forward their Eastern European policies. They blame their problems primarily on external forces. Their fear of West Germany, however, is mainly political rather than military. The propagandized military threat, however, can be used to discipline Eastern European states.

The Soviets are concerned about the impact of noncommunist ideology and subversion on the more exposed and receptive populations of Eastern Europe. Here the Soviets face the dilemma that either the granting of more liberality or a reversion to a tighter control from Moscow could add to tension and adversely affect the European equilibrium. Unfortunately for the Soviets, the ideal solution is the establishment of Soviet Republic in East Europe by annexation; but this "logical" solution is unrealistic and unattainable, at least for the predictable future.

The Soviet invasion of Czechoslovakia in August 1968 cannot be viewed as a turning point in Soviet foreign policy. It was a natural development of the policy objective of defending the status quo in Eastern Europe. It is viewed by the Soviets as mostly an internal question rather than a question of Soviet foreign policy. Still, the decision may have been influenced by the expected withdrawal of the United States from Vietnam, such favorable trends as the possible future withdrawal of American forces from Western Europe, and the changing strategic military balance. In a sense, it was uncharacteristic in that it represented a major decisive act—the first such forceful act of will in the post-Khrushchev era.

Where may this lead? In the short term, the Soviets seek to insulate what has occurred in Czechoslovakia. The prospect of the future use of force against another Eastern European state, say Rumania, appears remote at this time but has not been eliminated.

Regarding Eastern Europe, however, there is uncertainty as to what is permissible in the way of reform. At what point would the Soviets intervene? The answer can vary from month to month. The degree of reform permitted is apparently related to Soviet confidence in the reliability and strength of indigenous leadership and the effectiveness of party and police control.

Even with a Soviet policy of co-existence towards Western Europe, the future can be increasingly dangerous. The internal factor of chauvinism, previously discussed, and the continued image of a threatening

Western Europe point to a dangerous trend. Also, weak and uncertain Western leadership encourages Soviet belief in the fulfillment of the prophetic doctrine of capitalist decadence. The Soviets still seek the destruction of the Atlantic Alliance and the elimination of the U.S. presence in Europe.

Relations with China   In projecting Soviet relations with Eastern Europe, consideration must be given to the influence of Communist China on these relations. This influence is strengthened by Soviet awareness of the Chinese Communist development of more sophisticated delivery systems for their growing stocks of nuclear weapons. It is limited, however, by Soviet confidence in their present overall military superiority over Communist China. Another limiting factor is ideological. China can hardly be considered an ally of the "revisionist" forces seeking a change in Eastern Europe.

Acerbated Soviet relations with Communist China can encourage the Soviets to secure their western flank by tighter controls. This was indicated in the Czech crisis in 1968. Also, states of Eastern Europe that are under pressure and are seeking more independence may turn to Peking for support. Difficulties in Eastern Europe can also be a factor leading to Soviet efforts to negotiate with the Chinese over Far Eastern borders and to improve relations with the Chinese leaders. A new initiative in this direction occurred during Kosygin's visit to Peking in the summer of 1969. The Soviets must accept that they lost the internal Chinese Communist power struggle with the definite fall of Liao Shou Chi. They may work for the day when new Chinese leaders with more regard for a rapprochement with Moscow can contend for power.

Reconciliation between the Soviet Union and China, however, could have some dangerous aspects for the U.S.S.R. If the Chinese return to a more moderate line and a reconciliation within the communist movement, they could play a more disruptive role in Eastern Europe and among Western European communist parties.

The Soviets still worry more about possible collusion between the United States and Communist China or between China and the Federal Republic of Germany. A future Soviet-U.S. crisis or a Sino-Soviet crisis then might be exploited against the Soviet interests. Looking far ahead, the Soviets may estimate that one billion Chinese with nuclear weapons could become a great danger to Siberia. They may worry about the long-term demographic threat. The Chinese might exploit politically the discontents within Soviet Central Asia and create problems for the Soviets in India.

While genuine Soviet concern about Communist China can generally not be gainsaid, Soviet leaders manipulate such concerns for political advantage.

1969 World Conference of ∪nist Parties

The 1969 World Conference of Communist Parties held in Moscow was only a limited success for the Soviets. First, the conference occurred after protracted efforts by the Soviet Union to gain support for the meeting. Second, of the 75 worker and communist parties represented, only eight of the 14 communist parties in power sent delegates. Third, the final statement agreed to by the conferees concerning the duty of parties towards their own working class, as well as to the international working class movement, represented a meaningless compromise. It was a vague formula that provided only a semblance of approval by the world communist movement for the Brezhnev doctrine of limited sovereignty in the Socialist Commonwealth.

Brezhnev's limited success at the conference was attributable in part to previous meetings such as the 1969 conference in Budapest. At that conference, other parties indirectly agreed not to discuss the invasion of

Czechoslovakia. The Soviets' success, however, was success by exhaustion—the end of a long process. It represented a large measure of agreement on the smallest possible area.

The Soviets were subsequently successful, however, in that the Western European communist parties have now put the Czech crisis in the background, although 16 of these parties, including the larger ones in Western Europe, previously denounced the Soviet Union's action against Czechoslovakia.

Still, the conference created certain embarrassments for the Soviet Union. The objective of the conference from the Soviet viewpoint was to obtain as much party support as possible for the Soviet's position concerning China. Yet an anti-Chinese statement was excluded from the conference conclusions. This Soviet concession concerning the anti-Chinese statement was required to get other parties to agree to a compromise formula of solidarity.

The conference also showed the world the divisions that persist in the communist movement. Left unresolved was the question of the relative priority of each party's responsibility to its own working class versus its responsibility to the international working class movement. The Soviets continue to assert that the duty is to the international working class, which means to the Soviet Union, as well as to each country's own working class. This position is not acceptable to a large number of the world Communist parties.

The crisis in the communist movement revealed by the Czech crisis and the subsequent 1969 World Conference continues. It is a crisis of confidence. The image of the U.S.S.R. remains damaged. The continuing Soviet problem is how to keep control of parties and to reinforce acceptance of Moscow's leadership of the world communist movement.

American
Panel
Findings

The economic position of the U.S.S.R. will continue to have considerable influence on the tendencies of the political leadership toward relatively moderate or hard line policies at home and abroad. Obviously, therefore, the economy's position will directly and indirectly affect the Soviet's policy.

The weakness of the economy is basically a problem of the system. It is not efficient enough to provide Soviet leaders with the resources needed to carry out the policies they have formulated. Specifically, a Stalinist-type central planning system is unable to provide automatic institutional reactions to new situations. Communist analysis says the economy has moved from extensive to intensive growth, but in fact, it is coming face to face with the problem of managing technological change and innovation. The inability of a centrally planned economy to respond to the demand for innovation hinders its overall advance to industrial maturity. Thus, a weak and divided leadership is faced with some difficult decisions.

A major dilemma currently facing the leadership, for example, is whether to heed the Army's demand for increased resources to develop ballistic missile capability or to enlarge consumer industries. The latter choice would not only provide material incentives for the work force, but also would release some of the 40 per cent of the work force still tied down to agricultural production.

The Soviet leadership must exercise judgment in three main areas of resource allocation: the investment for basic economic growth, the attempt to satisfy rising consumer expectations, and the effort to meet military needs. Since large military outlays in recent years have slowed the overall economic growth rate, concern has been expressed within the Soviet leadership regarding the size of such outlays. A reduction in future programs would, among other things, have a direct bearing on strategic arms talks with the U.S.

The choice of priorities in the Soviet economy, between security and economic growth, has been discussed frequently in Soviet professional journals, including the military periodicals. Even so, the panel emphasizes that, in spite of certain constraints on the economy in recent years, the rate of growth has been quite respectable and military funding has in fact increased.

Leadership Struggles at the Top

The view has been expressed that placing undue emphasis on which leader does what is not a useful exercise. There are some indications that individuals concerned with administering the economy tend to shy away from policy lines that were characteristic of Stalin more than do those in the security apparatus, the police, and the military. The impact of the domestic policies' repression on the intelligentsia, the writers and poets, therefore, does not concern Soviet leaders as much as a similar alienation of factory directors and chief engineers.

Some panelists think that the present generation of leaders in the Soviet Union is the most mediocre ever; that is, that they have come up through the system and are in fact a mass of faceless bureaucrats.

The relationship between the armed forces and the party will surely command the attention of analysts in the next few years. The role of the military in 1964 when Khrushchev was dropped seems to indicate that no political leader can rely on support from the armed forces merely on the grounds of having provided the usual patronage rewards of jobs and promotions.

Since the current military leadership benefited from the Stalinist purges in the late 1930's it is not likely to resist the moves toward restoring some aspects of policies that were characteristic of Stalin and the glorification of Stalin carried out by the party. Such a pattern of party activity should, of course, favor the military by resulting in larger allocations for defense spending.

National Interests v. Ideology in Foreign Policy Current Soviet foreign policy seeks to create favorable international conditions for the construction of socialism and communism in concert with a general downgrading of the concept of peaceful coexistence. The panelists think that present Soviet foreign policy is not so much directed against the United States or Western Europe as toward other socialist countries. In fact, the disciplining of socialist countries has become not only the cardinal issue but also an Achilles' heel for Soviet leaders.

The Soviet hard line directed towards Bonn is due in some respects to the success of West Germany's *Ostpolitik.* The Kremlin seeks its own ends in West Germany through indirect maneuvers aimed at achieving a relationship similar to the one with Finland, in which public opinion and diplomacy influence noncommunist policy makers to move in a prescribed fashion. The efforts by the Soviets to promote this concept have not been very astute, since an early aim on their part clearly must be ejection of the United States from West Germany. If the American troops were to leave the center of Europe, an effort at accommodation with the Soviet Union by Western Europeans could be expected to follow.

Some panel members emphasized the continuation of developments characteristic of the Stalinist period in the Soviet Union, which they felt endangered all of

Western Europe, not just West Germany. Resultant policies permit only a small degree of limited coexistence at best, and then only as it favors Soviet interests.

As far as arms talks are concerned, it is felt that the Soviet Union would endeavor to gain a tacit agreement with the United States that both countries are now, in fact, strategic equals.

When the panel sought to distinguish elements shaping foreign policy decisions, the following questions arose: In considering the Soviet Union, is there, in fact, a question of ideology versus national interest? Or is there a duality of Marxist-Leninist internationalism, on the one hand, and a narrow Russian nationalism on the other? Is the formulation and implementation of foreign policy an attempt to reconcile this dualism of inconsistent ideological commitments? The Panelists conclude that the resulting conflict of interests within the Soviet leadership and the subsequent attempts at reconciliation explain the uncertain and inconsistent nature of Moscow's foreign policy.

Restalinization: its Characteristics and Effects

With varying degrees of dissent, it is agreed that "restalinization" is the most decisive development in the Soviet Union since 1964. Thus, the downfall of Khrushchev is interpreted as being nearly as important as the death of Stalin, with opposite consequences, of course. Domestically, "restalinization" has had several consequences: It has affected cultural policies; it has allowed the upgrading of the secret police and the increase in the number of concentration camps; it has led to the re-evaluation of Stalin; and it has resulted in the toning down of economic reforms. The praise of Stalin by the current leadership is described as a strategic, long-term policy as opposed to a tactical, or a short-term tightening up pattern. Furthermore, nearly all the destalinization doctrines have been dropped, including the theoretical concepts of the state of the whole people, the Party of the whole people, socialist legality, and the peaceful transition to socialism.

Certain panelists are, however, reluctant to use "restalinization" as an overall term to describe events in the Soviet Union. Of course, there is a visible tightening of social control by the leaders. To define this as "restalinization," however, could hinder a clear perspective of Soviet development and tend to induce a cyclical analysis in describing events. The view of some panelists is that in following a cyclical pattern of analysis (or appearing to do so), there is a tendency to overlook the dynamics of a system caught up in the process of political development. The panel poses the question: Is the process a symbolic manipulation of Stalin's image to force the populace back into line with the threat of what could happen? The length of Stalin's shadow, one panelist suggests, may provide a figurative thermometer of the general line of politics in the U.S.S.R.

In the process of seeking an adequate framework for viewing Soviet policies, it is pointed out that the label "restalinization," is clumsy. The term does not mean a complete reversion to Stalinism, of course. But it does imply, according to one panelist, that the regime accepts unavoidable economic reform while maintaining control in all possible spheres. Yet the return to elements of Stalinism differs from Stalinism of the past on at least three counts: No mass terror; A selective cult of personality rather than the cult of one man and; A policy of repression along ideological and cultural lines accompanied by attempts to calm the mass of the people with material satisfactions.

Although ideology as such is declining as an instrument of political power, the rhetoric of Marxism-Leninism is used increasingly by party leaders as a basis for maintaining their minority-controlled monopoly of political power.

In the use of ideology, there has been a shift away from an appeal to the outside world and a trend toward an aggressive defensiveness. Since such theories as limited sovereignty and peaceful counter-revolution have received prominence, all mild reforms have been pushed aside because they bring accusations of counter-revolutionary policies. Particular emphasis has been placed on patriotic efforts, such as glorification of wars, as well as a toning down of the self-criticism of the Stalin era.

Panel members point out that the process of isolating segments of society has bred pockets of opposition, most markedly among the intelligentsia who resist the cultural crackdown by passing underground manuscripts from reader to reader. Why doesn't the leadership simply put a stop to this? Because outside influences, namely the parties of Eastern Europe and the world communist movement, exert significant restraints on the Kremlin. For instance, that people do talk back in court and are heard doing so on the outside, and that illegal literature circulates widely in the country and outside as well, demonstrate that pre-1953 trends were not being resumed in toto in 1969.

The panel's task was not only to reflect but to judge whether the Soviet Union could successfully move through this period of transition. The question is thus posed: Is this problem of such scope or dimension to affect the efficiency of the Soviet state in the way it gets along in the world? There is some thought that the gap between expectation and performance may bring about a kind of "palace revolution," similar to the events between January and August 1968, the period prior to the invasion of Czechoslovakia. There is general panel agreement that this pattern of Soviet domestic politics cannot go on indefinitely. It is clear, however, that while outsiders can outline the dynamics of the situation, they are unable to predict a schedule for possible reaction.

Although Soviet leaders have a history of being rather selective in the use of their ideology, observers believe that the Kremlin would view the collapse of any socialist state as having disastrous consequences for the whole socialist system including the Soviet Union.

The Soviet leaders are concerned with developments in other socialist countries because any political, economic or social change confronts them with the prospects of accepting the legitimacy of the change and living with its implications at home. Therefore, when shifts of policy occur, the Kremlin feels the need to take drastic measures—as in Czechoslovakia—just as Stalin was moved to read the Yugoslav party out of the bloc. Although the leadership cannot accept a deviant socialism of the kind exhibited in Prague, a subservient Czech regime in turn exerts an economic drain on Moscow, posing a real dilemma for the Kremlin.

Six points were put before the panel and generally accepted as current Soviet thinking about Eastern Europe: 1.) Changes in war technology have made the area less important militarily to the Soviet Union in 1970 than it was in 1944 or 1945, although a psychological fear of West Germany remains; 2.) The German Democratic Republic is viewed as a wasting asset, in view of the cost involved in maintaining Ulbricht and in contrast to the comparative success of West Germany's *Ostpolitik;* 3.) Economic liabilities of Eastern Europe, such as the cost of extracting raw materials and the shoddy quality of manufactured goods, may tie the region to the Soviet Union, but do not bring the full economic return that would result if the raw material were marketed in Western Europe; 4.) The more stable a communist regime becomes, the more it tends to be revisionist and independent; consequently, establishment of a communist regime is no guarantee of dependable pro-Soviet orientation; 5.) The emergence of an ideological heresy in Eastern Europe can pose a political liability inside the Soviet Union; 6.) The continuing ferment among cultural groupings throughout Eastern Europe carries a far-reaching effect on the ethnic groups within the Soviet Union.

Concerning the economic strain of supporting external "liberation" movements and preparing for conventional war, there is panel disagreement only as to degree. It is noted that Eastern Europe does not carry some of the burden of the Vietnam War. Discussion continues in the Soviet Union concerning conventional war as well as nuclear exchanges, thus underscoring the military usefulness of Eastern Europe even today.

The panel feels that Soviet sensitivity toward the German Democratic Republic will not go to the extreme of, say, supplying atomic weapons to Ulbricht, although the economic successes of West Germany do present problems for Moscow, East Germany and Poland.

Limited sovereignty, a doctrine originally contained in the Declaration of the 81 Communist Parties in December 1960, was largely overlooked until the invasion of Prague. It was then widely publicized, but proved difficult to apply except by sheer military force. It perhaps can work effectively with a Quisling regime, but if no such leadership can be found, the doctrine becomes an embarrassment to its propagators. Limited sovereignty was basically not a reaction to the Prague reforms but a continuation of a long ideological process.

The concept of limited sovereignty is considered an article of faith, a clear guide for Soviet action, applicable to domestic as well as foreign policies.

The economic reforms that the Hungarians have carried out are at least as radical as the recent Czech efforts. The Hungarians have also done some quiet experimentation in the political field. They have, for example, restored the single member constituency traditional to Hungarian politics, and are moving toward having three candidates, all of them reliable Party members of course, in each district. Especially noticeable in the Hungarian press since August 21, 1968, is the constant repetition by everybody, including Kadar after he came out of his three-week, self-imposed isolation, that "we are going ahead with the economic reforms."

Yugoslavia seems to be caught on the horns of a dilemma. On the one hand, the Yugoslavs recognize that while now doubly vulnerable from a geopolitical standpoint, as long as they maintain even a residual commitment to socialism they are, like it or not, a suitable model (at least potentially) for emulation in Eastern Europe. On the other hand, they govern as primary beneficiaries of a single-party system and derive authority from that system by a commitment to socialism. In developing their domestic and foreign policies, there is no external reference to judge just how far they can go.

The Warsaw Pact and COMECON are no longer viewed as instruments of control between Moscow and Eastern Europe. The Warsaw Pact is not because more nationals of different states are being given top command positions; COMECON is not because it has failed to enforce the doctrine of socialist international division of labor, and because joint companies and cross-frontier investments have been relatively meaningless. Operating in parallel to these more formal structures, and, in fact, exercising great political control, are the political contracts operating through multilateral meetings of party leaders, the regular meetings of party commissions, and the regular ideological exchanges of party organizations.

The panel agrees that the Soviet leaders are grappling with a many-sided problem in Eastern Europe, and must consequently employ various means to maintain their hold—including multilateral instruments of control, as well as the burden, politically and economically, of keeping troops in Eastern Europe indefinitely. It is generally accepted by the panel that the types of controls now exercised by the Soviets over Eastern Europe cannot continue in the long run, at least in the same fashion as at present. Cited as evidences of continuing weaknesses in political control are the alienation of Eastern European youth despite efforts to indoctrinate them by party leaders, as well as the unrest among differing cultures in the regions.

The question of whether the Soviet Union would invade a country like Rumania would seem to hinge largely on whether a conflict elsewhere in the world were to occupy the attention of the major powers. Of course, any indication that the national party were becoming unable to discipline the population at large would bring Soviet troops quickly. In specific instances, it is noted that Hungary is limiting its reforms to the realm of economics and is not going as far as the Czechs did. The downfall of the latter's party leadership came when it drew political conclusions from economic reforms. The Soviets have used a kind of ostracism towards obstreperous parties, such as Yugoslavia's, by negatively influencing relations of other Eastern European parties to Belgrade. Ultimately, of course, what transpires in Eastern Europe hinges on changes within the Soviet leadership.

Guarded optimism exists concerning the ultimate shape of forces in Eastern Europe. It is based on the assumption that the Soviets would not be able to preserve the status quo indefinitely.

In dissenting from this optimism, some panelists cite the long-term nature of the "neostalinists' " policies, the buildup of political pressure over activities in Western Europe, and the divergences in the world communist movement ranging from restalinization to communist national revolutionary warfare and communist reform. The complexities of the world movement demand a flexible response by the noncommunist world and present the most far-reaching problem in the future.

Relations with China

The irrational Soviet preoccupation with China tends to place the real threat of Peking to Moscow beyond realistic perspective. A series of minor border conflicts obviously would pose no significant danger to the security of the Soviet state. Nonetheless, the irrational preoccupation decisively influences Moscow's attitude toward its western borders. The panel generally agrees that the Sino-Soviet dispute takes its greatest toll in Moscow's attempts to marshal the movement as a whole behind its position. No effort has been made to indicate what long-range effects the dispute would have on the straining toward independence by Eastern European parties. Some panelists believe that should the Chinese military establishment exert more power in the future, a closer tie with Moscow might result if for no other reason than that the Chinese need to obtain advanced technology and military hardware. Even if Chinese leadership does change, the weight of historical experience suggests it is unlikely that Soviet and Chinese leaders will ever settle into an easy working relationship.

PART TWO

The Background Paper

I.

Introduction

Soviet leaders today face a number of fundamental questions dating from the Khrushchev era that cannot remain unanswered indefinitely. It may prove impossible to resolve these problems without provoking a leadership crisis.

Khrushchev's successors inherited not only his policies but also the difficulties his policies created. For at least five months after he was deposed, it appeared that Moscow's policies corresponded to what Peking called "Khrushchevism without Khrushchev." Indeed, the similarities in policy between the Brezhnev-Kosygin regime and its predecessors remain greater than the differences. Nevertheless, although the point of departure for both policies is identical, Soviet leaders now confront an important point of decision.

Above all, the Soviet leaders must resolve the question of purpose. It is the loss of purpose that today divides the Soviet leadership and undermines the Soviet will to act in the face of new dangers and new opportunities. This is the fundamental source of the malaise and indecision that grip Soviet leaders. They must decide the recurring basic question in Soviet policy: The relative priorities of their direction of a powerful state versus their traditional role as leaders in the world Communist movement. As they extend Soviet power on a global scope, the Soviet leaders must decide whether to challenge U.S. influence everywhere in the process or to settle for limited gains and a more stable accommodation. Furthermore, they must decide whether to continue diverting scarce resources from internal growth in order to widen the range of foreign policy choices and achieve ambitious goals. Regardless of the decisions reached, the very fact of decision will affect the delicate internal social equilibrium and stir renewed factional conflict.

Substantial evidence suggests that the Soviet leadership is seriously divided over the occupation of Czechoslovakia. It continues to be wrenched by controversy on how to deal with varying degrees of opposition within the U.S.S.R. and Eastern Europe. The Soviet leadership appears to be divided along a continuum of policy views between these poles: At one extreme, advocacy of relaxing international tensions, retreat from overcommitments in foreign policy, and resolution of marginal international disputes through compromise and mutual concessions. At the other extreme, advocacy of a further buildup in Soviet military power leading to a measurable degree of strategic superiority, a direct challenge to the United States for global primacy, greater assistance to allies and clients, especially those under attack, and postponement of internal growth in the interests of strengthening national security and exploiting international opportunities.

It would be an overstatement to say those who favor the latter course are made up entirely of expansion-minded or ideologically oriented leaders, although both types are evident. Rather it is, on the whole, a group that feels Khrushchev needlessly surrendered the initiative to the United States. He is believed to have overestimated American capabilities and staying power, overlooked domestic contradictions within the U.S., and allowed many opportunities to slip by. This group is skeptical of U.S. intentions. It is inclined to believe that international stability works to the advantage of the noncommunist nations, not only by preserving the status quo, but also by undermining the Soviet position in Eastern Europe and within the international communist movement generally. Instead of eventual détente, this group foresees a continuous period of challenge and response between the two global powers, marked by periodic respites in the form of ad hoc arrangements and de facto stalemates. This group would probably make more concessions to achieve an ultimate reconciliation with China, thus removing the specter of Moscow's becoming the victim of a Sino-American understanding. Hence this group might be willing to run considerable risks aimed at mending relations with China, even though such steps retard or reverse progress toward détente with the United States.

It would, however, be an overstatement to say that those who favor the former course are willing to adjust the Soviet economy through extensive liberal reform, to retreat markedly from the precepts of Marxism-Leninism in Soviet internal affairs, or to concentrate on building communism in one country with an abandonment of global ambitions. Nevertheless, the group disposed toward international accommodation and concentration on internal priorities and ideological flexibility would be less disposed to sacrifice the burgeoning demands for increases in consumer well-being and increases in rates of economic growth. The Soviets disposed towards such beliefs might view international stability as a more favorable phenomenon and foresee the prospects of undermining the internal position of capitalist society through the forces presently at work, without running greater risks of direct confrontation. They might find greater satisfaction, too, in the achievements already obtained by the Soviet Union in redressing the strategic nuclear balance and building up more effective conventional forces.

Rational control of decision-making and pragmatic response to changing times would be favored by those who share such policy predispositions. Indicators of the relative strength of these predispositions and the competing factions involved are reflected in the stance taken by Soviet policy makers on key issues.

Within the U.S.S.R., the seemingly calm, controlled and rational demeanor of Khrushchev's two principal successors, Brezhnev and Kosygin, was viewed by many as a welcome reversal of an erratic pattern of behavior. For a time, the bland, bureaucratic, pragmatic personalities of present Soviet leaders seemed to correlate with their actions. The Czech crisis, however, made it apparent that the Brezhnev-Kosygin team represented not so much a unified and stable leadership as it did a latently explosive marriage of factional convenience, joining the partisans of Khrushchev's policies with his detractors.

II.

The Final Years of the Khrushchev Decade

On October 12, 1964, at a dramatic session of the ruling
Presidium of the Soviet Communist Party's (C.P.S.U.) Central
Committee, power changed hands in Moscow.

Nikita S. Khrushchev was dismissed from the posts of Central
Committee First Secretary and Chairman of the U.S.S.R. Council
of Ministers. His ouster from the center of authority was ratified
on October 13-14 at a plenary session of the C.P.S.U. Central
Committee. Leonid I. Brezhnev replaced him as chief of the more
influential party apparatus and Alexei N. Kosygin became head
of the governmental bureaucracy. The official announcement of
this unprecedented event in Soviet history—the bloodless removal
of the single leader of party and state—declared that the 70-year-
old Khrushchev had resigned "in view of his age and deteriorated
health." Foreign observers rejected this explanation when a
Pravda editorial, on October 17, indirectly but unmistakably accused Khrushchev of "plan-concocting, scheming, immature and
hasty action, bragging" and "drift." Thereafter, an almost total
ban was imposed on mentioning Khrushchev's name in Soviet
media and his closest aides were demoted. Most important, the
policies that Khrushchev had championed toward the end of his
regime were soon discarded or redefined, and a new style of leadership emerged on the Soviet scene. An examination of Khrushchev's final policy moves and leadership style should, therefore,
precede inquiry into the behavior and outlook of the present
regime.

In the field of internal politics, one of the most drastic steps
taken by Khrushchev was his great reorganization of the Communist party apparatus. This closely-unified structure, manned by
upwards of 500,000 general organizers and ideological specialists,

had long served the ranking political hierarchy as an instrument for its nearly absolute domination over society. In November 1962, Khrushchev made public his scheme to divide the party apparatus into industrial and agricultural sections. The reorganization was ostensibly designed to improve party "guidance" of state technical experts in charge of the country's factories and farms. In reality, party officials were driven to perform functions of operational management beyond their qualifications and inclinations. The reorganization, it became clear, was instigated for the purpose of introducing, on a crash basis, various technological innovations that were unacceptable to professionally-minded state administrators. (The grandiose chemical program for industry and special cropping patterns in agriculture are prime examples.)

A major consequence of the reorganization was an undermining of party discipline and authority. The jurisdictions of bureaucratic agencies became more confused than usual and the interventions of party functionaries into economic life became more difficult. At the same time, the party propaganda network was ordered to concentrate on technical rather than doctrinal themes. The overall effect of Khrushchev's reorganization thus was a visible and potentially grave weakening of the party's totalitarian control over life and thought in the U.S.S.R.

Other important changes swiftly followed. These involved the whole planning mechanism, the administrations of the republics and local governments, and state and party organs in agriculture. The ability of party secretaries to intervene in industry was impaired by the amalgamation of some economic regions in 1962-63.

Khrushchev, meanwhile, supported changes in the system of economic planning and management. The conceptual basis was laid in a *Pravda* article by Professor E. Liberman urging new profit and sales criteria for the management of Soviet enterprises.

Action did not match rhetoric, however, as Khrushchev applied the new management criteria. Although managers were told sales and profits were to be added as measures of their success, physical output and inflexible directives were kept in force. The equivocal nature of these Khrushchev-sponsored changes, which tended to blur requirements and confuse lines of authority, hardly contributed to increased economic efficiency.

Khrushchev's virulent criticism of Stalin's harsh methods of rule set in motion a process of limited relaxation of dictatorial rule in the Soviet Union and the European communist states. Khrushchev vilified the memory of Stalin, in part to open a political safety-valve and gain personal popularity. The anti-Stalin campaigns, begun in 1956 and pursued thereafter in stop-and-go fashion, were also linked with Khrushchev's general political conception, which was partly innovative and partly pragmatic. His desire to revise time-honored practices seemed to require that an effort be made to discredit Stalin, the towering symbol of orthodox communism.

Not surprisingly, misgivings about destalinization were widespread in the ranks of the Soviet bureaucracy. Typical were the remarks of General A. A. Yepishev, chief of the Main Political Administration of the Soviet Army and Navy, at the Central Committee meeting in June 1963. Yepishev's speech, which was not published in its entirety until July 1964, featured a denunciation of "those who under the pretense of struggle with the cult of the individual (i.e., Stalinism) come out against the foundations of organization and against authorities in the life of society." It later became apparent that many others, who shared Yepishev's background of work in the party and the secret police, agreed that destalinization was loosening the bonds of social discipline throughout the Soviet orbit.

In September 1964, Khrushchev questioned the rightfulness of maintaining the Stalinist order of national priorities that emphasized basic and military industries. In his address to a gathering of senior political and economic officials on the next Five-Year Plan, the Premier boasted that "the country's defense is at the proper level." Khrushchev's speech, summarized in *Pravda* on October 2, 1964, indicated that for the sake of improving economic performance and lifting the morale of the workers, he was ready to shift the pattern of resource allocation more to the advantage of the long-neglected consumer. He even went so far as to raise the possibility of economizing on military spending.

The psychological groundwork for such a turn of investment policy had been laid by Khrushchev's frequent attacks on the austere "metal-eaters" in the regime's higher councils.

Under Khrushchev, the priority during the late 1950s shifted away from the military and toward modernization of Soviet energy, metal-working, and transportation industries. Whereas industrial investment grew by 11.6 percent in the 1952-55 period and 12.8 percent through 1960, the increase in defense spending over the same span was negligible—an average of less than 0.5 percent annually. The growth in GNP during these same two periods was a very respectable 7.0 and 6.5 percent. During the same period, the total number of men under arms was reduced from above 5 million to close to 3 million. Although defense rose in sharp response to the first Kennedy budget in 1961, the principle of shifting priorities had been set.

During 1960-1963, the substantial increase in the annual growth of defense coincided with a decline in the capital investment rate to 4.8 percent. GNP grew an average of only 4 percent annually. Although the poorer economic performance was in part a result of disastrous harvests, the slowdown in industrial growth seems a direct result of the diversion of resources to defense, away from investment in development of modern petroleum, metal processing and working, and chemical industries.

Following the economic slowdown of 1960-1963, the pendulum again swung away from defense priority—defense spending fell behind the overall growth rate of GNP, which was about 7 percent in 1963-1965. This may have been a factor in the timing of Khrushchev's fall, for October is the time of year when key economic decisions are made.

The Kremlin's foreign policy in 1963-64 was moving in a direction which suggested official recognition of the Soviet public's interest in peaceful national development. After many years of inconclusive negotiations, the conclusion of a partial nuclear test ban treaty with Washington and London appeared to symbolize Moscow's willingness to inaugurate a period of limited accommodation with the western democracies. In July 1964, Khrushchev's son-in-law A. I. Adzhubei toured the Federal Republic of Germany, a European policy initiative that reportedly disturbed the intransigent communist rulers of East Germany. Upon returning to Moscow, Adzhubei wrote a number of enthusiastic articles about prospects for trade and cultural ties with Bonn. On September 3, it was announced that Khrushchev would visit West Germany.

In his policy toward Eastern Europe, Khrushchev had become relatively tolerant of forces leaning toward national self-assertion and independence of the Yugoslav variety. The Soviet chief's reliance on multilateral consultations and bargaining had failed to push forward his 1962 scheme for uniformity via a supranational planning body in the Council for Mutual Economic Assistance (C.M.E.A.—COMECON). Only slight progress was made toward the goals of national specialization of production and cooperation in scientific and technical research. The same was true of joint projects because of balance-of-payments difficulties and national preferences of self-sufficiency. Due, in part, to the lagging cooperation of the members, the Eastern group of nations was producing at least 10 percent less of the world's industrial production than planned in 1960, and growth rates for industrial production were declining. In April 1964, against this backdrop of worsening strain within COMECON, Rumanian President Gheorghiu-Dej flatly asserted the right to determine his own economic and foreign policy line. Rumanian-West German trade had increased substantially between 1960 and 1964, and Bucharest now responded positively to President Lyndon Johnson's call for the "building of bridges" between the United States and Eastern Europe. An agreement was signed enabling Rumania to acquire industrial equipment from the United States with credits to be guaranteed by the Export-Import Bank. The way seemed to be opening for a major expansion of U.S. trade with Eastern Europe, then running at only $200 million, a volume far below Western Europe's almost $5 billion shipments to the East.

Simultaneously with this trend toward normalization of relations within the Soviet bloc, Khrushchev ardently tried to discredit and isolate the Chinese communists, who in Stalinist fashion, preached the necessity of totally mobilizing human and material resources. Khrushchev's last months in office were marked by the rallying of support for a world communist conference that would endorse a more refined sort of Marxism-Leninism and presumably formalize the widening rift between European and Asian branches of the movement.

The style of leadership Khrushchev exemplified marked a clear discontinuity with the Stalinist past. Khrushchev openly ridiculed Stalin's cloistered mode of life and his failure to learn at first hand the actual situation in the country. In contrast, Khrushchev flamboyantly inspected every corner of the Soviet Union and often made extravagant promises that could only arouse hopes of material prosperity among the population. His much-publicized foreign tours whetted the nation's appetite for foreign contacts and new ideas. At the same time, Khrushchev— ironically, like Stalin in the 1930s—began to set himself above the party's governing bodies. More and more, he failed to consult with a dozen or so senior colleagues in the party Presidium when making statements and planning foreign trips, and the 175 members of the Central Committee, representing vested organizational and philosophical interests. The Committee seemed on the verge of completely losing its ability to shape high policy.

III.

The Rise of the Soviet Military-Industrial-Apparatus Complex

The character of the post-Khrushchev regime was foreshadowed by policy and personnel shifts ratified at the C.P.S.U. Central Committee meeting on November 16, 1964. After a secret report by Presidium member and Central Committee Secretary Nikolai V. Podgorny, Khrushchev's party reorganization was annulled and the separate party committees for industry and agriculture were merged. The party press deplored Khrushchev's reorganization as a hasty enterprise that resulted in "confusion of the functions, rights and duties of party, Soviet and managerial agencies." It had violated the established rule of the division of labor between party controllers and state executives, and "pushed party committees into replacement of managerial agencies." Khrushchev's notion of a technically-functional party apparatus instead of a totalitarian-controlling mechanism was censured in the Stalinist idiom as "commercialism" and "pure empiricism." The party's internal system of political indoctrination was once more to lay stress upon doctrinal and historical themes rather than practical economics.

An important promotion was made at the November 1964 meeting. Alexander N. Shelepin, a politically flexible but ideologically rigid career party *apparatchik,* was elevated to full membership in the Presidium. Shelepin was named first secretary of the Young Communist League *(Komsomol)* in November 1952, when Stalin was grooming new cadres to take positions about to be vacated through a massive purge. In 1958, he became chairman of the Committee for State Security (K.G.B.), and the following year his speech to the 21st Party Congress was so intolerant of dissent as to merit censorship in the offices of *Pravda.* At the 22nd Party Congress in 1961, Shelepin proposed a new drive against the "internal enemy." He was soon released from the secret police directorship and appointed chairman of a new U.S.S.R. Party-State Control Committee.

P. N. Demichev, another ideologically orthodox functionary, made the second largest gain in the wake of Khrushchev's ouster. He was awarded candidate membership in the party Presidium. Demichev, the future deputy of Brezhnev in charge of cultural affairs, sharply rebuked intellectual nonconformists from the platform of the 22nd Congress, denouncing "certain immature writers, artists, and composers, foremost young people" who had "succumbed to such illnesses as false innovation and formalism." He also assailed "some important men of letters and art" who "fearing to seem old-fashioned, flirt with such 'seekers of novelty' and humor them." Others promoted at the November 1964 Central Committee meeting included General Yepishev and V. Ye. Semichastny, K.G.B. chairman, who were raised from candidacy to full membership in the Committee. These organizational changes were matched by a series of press articles that refurbished the image of the K.G.B. Semichastny's own contribution to this process was an article in *Pravda* of May 4, 1965, that glossed over the crimes of Stalin's policemen and praised Soviet intelligence agents for their valuable and "honorable work in the struggle with the enemy."

These personnel shifts seemed to establish Brezhnev as the dominant personality in the new hierarchy, not so much because the new appointees were his followers or cronies, but rather because they formed an alliance with the conservative wing of the Khrushchevite faction which he led. Kosygin and Mikoyan emerged as the leaders of the liberal wing of the erstwhile Khrushchev coalition. Thus, while both Brezhnev and Kosygin represented the middle, each leaned in a different direction. Although both might muster effective majorities when in agreement, each was under varying degrees of pressure coming from different and frequently opposing directions. The factional equilibrium shifted further toward the conservative pole with the retirement of A. I. Mikoyan as titular chief of state and his replacement by Podgorny, whose past enthusiasm for Khrushchev's domestic and foreign policies was clearly inferior to that of his predecessor. Shelepin's Party-State Control Committee was dissolved at the same time, which served to strengthen Brezhnev, but did not alter the factional balance.

The most conspicuous consequence of the factional shifts in the Soviet leadership was the enhanced power of those representing the traditional military, heavy industry, and the conservative elements in the party apparatus. These three forces, which shared many interests and had suffered most under Khrushchev, constituted a sort of informal military-industrial-apparatus complex. Party reorganization and relaxation of ideological controls had weakened and undermined the conservative and career party functionaries. The policy of détente resulted in trimming the size and status of the traditional military and seemed to expose the country to serious vulnerabilities. The reorganization and decentralization of the economy created serious problems for all three elements of this coalition.

The Escalation of Military Expenditures

The influence of the Soviet military-industrial-apparatus in the new post-Khrushchev regime manifested itself early. Although overt military expenditures at first were to decline by 3.8 percent (500 million rubles) following the change in leadership, the new budget included large increases in spending in categories generally believed to harbor military research and development. The Institute for Strategic Studies (London) later estimated that in 1965 Soviet military costs rose by as much as $5-10 billion over the level fixed by Khrushchev for 1964. These additions to military spending may have been decided in mid-1965 when spokesmen for the regime underlined the gravity of the international situation and denounced the Johnson Administration for escalating the war in Vietnam.

Increases in military spending were accompanied by open repudiation of Khrushchev's views on military organization, military technology and strategic doctrine. In January 1965, I. P. Prusanov, writing in the historical magazine of the Central Committee's Institute of Marxism-Leninism, stated that "The Party

has cautioned against premature and arbitrary conclusions . . ."
and specifically pointed out:

> That kind of tendency made itself known in recent years.
> Some comrades only recently expressed the thought that
> in conditions of the current day development of military
> technology, the Air Force and Navy have supposedly lost
> their former importance. This conclusion is at variance
> with one of the most important postulates of Soviet mili-
> tary doctrine concerning the harmonious development of
> all branches and services of the Armed Forces.

The military doctrine of using combined arms was also
treated in the Defense Ministry newspaper, *Red Star,* on January 24. Marshal M. V. Zakharov, a 66-year-old specialist on land
warfare, was reappointed chief of the General Staff, a post he had
held from 1960-63. Zakharov's writings are notable for the emphasis put on strict professionalism in formulating military theory
and the folly of reposing blind faith in a single weapons system.

Further changes in allocations and priorities were revealed
by Brezhnev at the Central Committee Plenum of March 24-26,
1965, when a new five-year program was announced to overcome
productive stagnation in the countryside. During the discussion of
Brezhnev's report, the priority of military claims on national resources was recognized. While an increase in farm prices was
authorized as an incentive for the peasants, Soviet investment in
agriculture grew much more slowly in 1966-67 than in 1961-65,
and at only about half the rate planned for 1966-70. This suggests that the military drain on the budget may have been a big
factor in retarding agricultural production.

The new regime's continuing concern with national security
problems and the pressures of the military was reflected in a
March 1965 decree of the Presidium of the Supreme Soviet that
recentralized the management of defense industries. The industries were removed from the control of territorial economic councils (Sovnarkhozy) and "State Committees", where they had been
placed by Khrushchev against the wishes of the professional military. Central ministries were reestablished for the aircraft, defense

technology, electronics, medium machinery, radio, and ship-building industries. A defense-oriented General Machinery Ministry was also reestablished under a long-time defense industry official. The influence of the military was further manifested during the same month when Marshal V. I. Chuikov, deputy minister of defense and member of the C.P.S.U. Central Committee, urged that a new organization, "Civil Defense" be created in place of local committees to guard effectively the entire country against enemy attack. This defense organization was later extended to Eastern Europe.

After 1965, the military received more than a proportionate share of resources. The U.S.S.R. Supreme Soviet meeting in December 1966 was told that the open defense budget for 1967 was 8 percent higher than the current year. (This figure appears intentionally misleading in view of the estimate of Western experts that the number of Soviet ICBMs rose from about 340 in 1966 to approximately 720 in 1967. The Institute for Strategic Studies' "Military Balance, 1967-1968" reports that in 1966 the Soviet leaders agreed to spend around $32 billion, or almost 9 percent of their gross national product, for defense needs.) At the time, December 1966, U.S. Secretary of Defense Robert S. McNamara announced the deployment of an antiballistic missile system around several Soviet cities. At the December 12-13 plenary session of the C.P.S.U. Central Committee, the steep rise of military outlays was justified by an ongoing "struggle against the forces of imperialism" and the necessity for a "further consolidation of our country's international positions." Politburo members spoke at many local party meetings on the topic of "the great-power, anti-Soviet policy of Mao Tse-tung and his group," which had entered into "a new and dangerous phase."

From 1965-1967, it is now estimated that Soviet defense spending expanded at an annual rate of 7.9 percent compared with a GNP growth rate of 5.7 percent. Good weather and other favorable developments accounted for the improved economic performance. Some new investment and moderate reform measures also produced short-term gains. But the deferment of major investment programs to modernize Soviet industry and agriculture

ʿmeant the problem of long-term economic growth had also been deferred to future years.

Direct costs for the upkeep of armed forces rose by 15 percent in 1968, and once more exceeded the previous year's figure supplied in the total published budget. An 11 percent increase in spending for science indicated an additional growth of military investment. The inconsiderable goal set for "capital investment," the major non-military consumer of machinery and equipment, and the ambitious target fixed for total machinery output also struck foreign analysts of the Soviet's 1968 economic plan. The 10th annual report of the Institute for Strategic Studies, "The Military Balance, 1968-1969," estimates that the U.S.S.R. in 1967 earmarked $50 billion for military use, or $18 billion more than was allotted the previous year. The Soviet Union, therefore, was making a greater defense effort in proportion to gross national product than the United States. Indeed, if Washington's spending directly on the Vietnam war is excluded, the amount of funds allocated to Soviet defenses roughly equalled the American level.

The Military Moves to Rehabilitate Stalin

The repudiation of Khrushchev's views on military doctrine was soon coupled with a repudiation of his assessment of Stalin as a military leader. Beginning with the celebration of the 20th anniversary of VE Day, a gradual rehabilitation of Stalin as a wartime leader assumed definite shape. It should be emphatically noted that this was a rehabilitation of *Stalin,* not *Stalinism.* It was restricted to his wartime leadership and not extended to his policies generally. Many inside the Soviet Union and outside viewed this rehabilitation with alarm and anxiety, fearful that it might be but a prelude to a full-scale restoration of Stalinism. Mindful of these fears, the Soviet leaders proceeded cautiously and selectively in their reassessment of Stalin, but they nevertheless proceeded, and the process is continuing. There is evidence suggesting that Stalin's rehabilitation met with some opposition and disapproval, and that the Soviet leadership remains divided on the issues of Stalin himself and the process and consequences of destalinization.

It is noteworthy, however, that the Soviet military saw a

definite advantage in resurrecting Stalin and associating itself with his wartime leadership. So did partisans of heavy industry and members of the conservative wing of the party apparatus. Prominent spokesmen for the traditional military took the lead in the dictator's rehabilitation. On April 28, 1965, Marshal I. S. Konev recalled Stalin's "positive role" during World War II as "chairman of the State Defense Committee and supreme commander-in-chief." On the following day, *Pravda* disavowed the one-sided presentation of events involving Stalin that was characteristic of military history under Khrushchev. Brezhnev paid unusual homage to Stalin's military leadership at the VE Day ceremonies on May 8. As in Stalin's day, the possibility of non-nuclear war in Europe was raised by U.S.S.R. Minister of Defense R. Ya. Malinovsky during a speech on May 14, the anniversary of the Warsaw Treaty Organization.

Since then, Stalin's wartime leadership has been consistently praised by Soviet marshals and generals, most recently in the extremely favorable assessment offered by Marshal Zhukov in his memoirs. Not only did Marshal Zhukov seek to absolve Stalin of the bungling attributed to him by Khrushchev, but Khrushchev himself was harshly deprecated by name. Thus, Zhukov provides a portrait of Stalin totally at variance with that drawn by Khrushchev and completely consistent with those drawn by noncommunist statesmen and diplomats.

The Restoration of the Primacy of Heavy Industry and Defense Spending

The progressive rehabilitation of Stalin and the parallel recovery of power by the military-industrial-apparatus coalition within the Soviet hierarchy aroused fears on the eve of the 23rd Party Congress that a full-scale restoration of Stalinism was imminent. In a number of speeches and articles published during the summer of 1965, prominent military and party leaders pressed their demands for more rapid improvement of weapons technology and called upon the Soviet public to defer their natural desire for an improvement in the standard of living in the interests of national security. On June 2, 1965, Suslov told Bulgarian party officials that this sacrifice was required by the continuing threat of the imperialist powers, i.e., the United States:

> We would like the life of the Soviet people to improve at a faster rate. But we are forced to consider objective reality, which poses the necessity of significant expenditures on our national defense. . . . In conditions whereby imperialist powers pursue an arms race and unleash aggression in various parts of the world, our party and government must maintain the defense of the country on the highest level, constantly improving it. . . . All this, of course, demands from the Soviet people considerable material sacrifices [and] expenditure on defense of a considerable portion of the national income.

Similar statements of varying degrees of intensity were made by Soviet government and party leaders in Navy Day rallies on July 24, 1965. While Premier Kosygin restricted himself to saying, "The Communist Party, its Central Committee, and the Soviet Government consider their primary duty to be the strengthening of the defense of our country," Presidium member A. I. Kirilenko emphasized that the party and government: ". . . consider it to be their most important task to increase constantly the might of the socialist state, to strengthen our armed forces, to provide them with the newest military technology and the most modern weapons." And Shelepin explicitly noted that this shift in priorities would be reflected in the next Five Year Plan:

> . . . the Central Committee and the Soviet government have devoted and will devote in the next Five-Year Plan unceasing attention to the further strengthening of the armed forces of the country, to the development of the defense industry.

In August this theme was reiterated by an editorial in the authoritative journal, *Kommunist,* coupled with an apology for diverting resources and investments away from the civilian sectors of the economy and a warning that any freeze or cutback in military spending was inappropriate under existing circumstances.

At the same time, the specialized military press featured

uncompromising statements. G. Miftiyev wrote in *Red Star* on June 4 of the "inevitably" growing importance of the armed forces' numerical strength, regardless of the fire-power of new weapons. On September 10, Major General A. Korniyenko, again in *Red Star,* upheld the primacy of military claims on national resources in spite of the "high costs" of maintaining an up-to-date military establishment. On November 19, Rocket and Artillery Forces Day, articles declared the need for all kinds of forces to assure victory in a nuclear age.

To be sure, spokesmen for the Soviet military-industrial-apparatus complex, as they pressed their demands for a modification of the resource allocations established during the Khrushchev era, encountered opposition within the leadership. Kosygin, Podgorny, and Polyansky, among others, periodically voiced claims that higher priority be given the domestic sector of the economy, but the varying degrees of emphasis given to the priority of heavy and defense industries by all spokesmen suggests that the consensus or majority was clearly on that side.

Brezhnev and Kosygin apparently occupied the middle ground in this controversy. Brezhnev leaned towards the military and heavy industry, while Kosygin veered toward those who felt defense and heavy industry were taking too large a share of the country's resources. One way out of this impasse appeared to be coupling the shift in priorities with long-needed economic reforms, which might boost production in the civilian sectors of the economy without requiring massive investment. Thus, the whole question of economic reform became enmeshed in the controversy over the allocation of resources. A consensus was reached whereby reforms would be selectively introduced into the economy in an effort to step up production and satisfy the needs and demands of the Soviet consumer through greater administrative efficiency.

The first steps in the Brezhnev-Kosygin regime's program of economic reforms were thrashed out at the Central Committee Plenum in September 1965. Some 28 centralized ministries, reminiscent of the Stalin period, were established to replace the 50 territorial economic councils *(Sovnarkhozy)* that Khrushchev had set up in 1957 for industrial management. A new system of planning, management, and incentives was to be introduced throughout Soviet industry during the period 1966-68, and throughout the public sector, except for collective farms (*kolkhozes*), by 1970. Enterprises converted to the new system were to be judged by measures such as gross sales, profit, and capital and labor productivity, rather than volume of output. A new organizational entity, the association, was added to encourage decentralization, autonomy of the enterprise, and efficiency.

The theory of the reform held promise of progress; its practical application failed. Most enterprises had no more control of inputs and outputs than in the past. The ministries retained control of such critical levers as pricing, wages, and supply. Supply prices were set, labor costs were given, and enterprises lacked the power to hire and fire. Investment was still centralized and incentives to adopt new technology were ineffective. The number of administratively allocated commodities remained high: the present total is about 20,000 items. The extent of central planning after the reform thus remains great.

Western specialists took note of the limited scope of the reform, which fell short of the hopes for decentralization aroused by Professor Liberman of Kharkov and other Soviet economists during the close of the Khrushchev era. The Brezhnev and Kosygin reforms represented the same contradictions and ambiguities as Khrushchev's, with a bit more elaborate articulation.

At the 23rd Party Congress, it became apparent that reforms would not affect the priority of heavy industry and defense industry. This policy was incorporated in the draft Five-Year Plan of economic development for 1966-70, which the 23rd Congress endorsed. An earlier survey of this document in *Pravda* had declared that the development of heavy industry was an "unshakeable commandment" and the party would never renounce "the interests of heavy industry and defense power." The new planning goal aimed at lifting the Soviet's steel output to virtually equal that of the United States by 1968, a goal that could not be met. (The Soviets produced 106.5 million metric tons in 1968; the U.S. 122 million.) The Soviet steel industry, of course, has been largely geared to defense needs. Brezhnev logically enough gave his backing to the cause of further military industrialization when he declared shortly after the 23rd Congress:

> An unchangeable principle of our economic policy was and remains the preponderant development of heavy industry as the basis of technical progress in all other branches of the national economy and the main foundation for strengthening the country's defense capability. . . . In present day conditions, our country is obliged to devote still more resources and attention to the strengthening of its defense power.

In late 1969 there appeared to be little sense of economic crisis among the Soviet leaders. Average to good growing weather helped boost the output of agriculture, and benefits from some of Khrushchev's innovations (as well as the absence of his disruptive policy of campaigns in economic planning), provided short-term stimulus. By early 1970, however, economic indices were dipping and drawing heavy public criticism.

The unsettled leadership seems disinclined to change economic procedures or priorities very drastically. So far the high-water mark of daring was reached in the September 1965 Plenum with the announcement of the Kosygin price reforms. Although this modest change may be viewed in historical perspective as the tip of an iceberg of new economic planning and management, that larger significance is conjectural today. Rather it appears that a "muddling through" divided leadership is making do in the economy. As long as the growth rate generally stays above 5 percent, this non-policy of inertia may continue (growth in 1966-68 was just above 5 percent). If, however, growth were to dip below 4 percent as it did in 1962 and 1963 with annual rates of 3.4 and 2.9 percent respectively and remain at such low rates for some time the leadership might be forced to stir itself to reallocate resources to investment and undertake meaningful economic reform.

The Buildup of Soviet Strategic Capabilities

Shortly before the 23rd Party Congress, Soviet commentators on military affairs extolled the underwater, round-the-world cruise of a fleet of Soviet nuclear submarines. In a six-week period it covered a distance of 24,000 nautical miles without surfacing. Official spokesmen pointed out the vessels' qualities of "concealment of approach to the launching position, high mobility and tremendous striking power."

Marshal Malinovsky, in his speech at the 23rd Congress, declared: "We calmly and securely stand on guard of our people's peaceful labor, especially now that the creation of the Blue Belt for Defense of our state has been completed." This remark was later elaborated upon by the East German Defense Minister, Army General Heinz Hoffmann, who in May 1966 told a group of East Berlin border guards: "The firm shield and sharp sword of the socialist military coalition are the rocket troops of the U.S.S.R., whose orbital, global, intercontinental, and medium-range rockets can carry a nuclear warhead with an explosive power of up to 100 megatons to every point on earth. To this are added the nuclear-powered submarines of the Blue Defense Belt, which can operate in every sea of the world."

Malinovsky informed the 23rd Congress that in a short span of time the Strategic Rocket Forces would be equipped with a large number of new pit-type and mobile launching installations. The Soviet observer A. Babakov later noted in his work, *The Soviet Army Today,* "The small-size solid fuel intercontinental missiles mounted on self-propelled caterpillar launching installations are already for launching. They cannot be detected either by spy satellites or air reconnaisance since they can easily change their launching positions." The air defense command, Malinovsky said, was equipped to destroy any hostile aircraft and numerous incoming missiles. In accord with the spirit of martial preparedness that ran through oratory at the 23rd Congress, a party and government decree adopted on May 7, 1966, ordered a vast increase of civil defense and paramilitary work. (The implementation of this decree was verified at conferences held in central party headquarters in April 1967 and June 1968 in the presence of party secretaries M. A. Suslov, D. F. Ustinov and A. I. Kirilenko.)

While the Soviet's steady buildup of strategic power received further impetus at the close of 1966, the diversification of Soviet military forces also proceeded apace. The death of Defense Minister Malinovsky in March was followed by rumors that a civilian replacement would be named with a view toward curtailing military influence in budgetary deliberations. On April 14 it was announced that the post of defense would be filled by Marshal Andrei Grechko, whose writings reflected unswerving belief in the traditional concept of operations by combined forces. The contingency of limited war in Europe between NATO and Warsaw Pact powers was brought up in July by the new Supreme Commander of Warsaw Pact Armies, U.S.S.R. First Deputy Defense Minister Marshal I. I. Yakubovsky. In the pages of *Red Star,* Yakubovsky cautioned against exaggerating the significance of nuclear weapons. Armor and artillery, he said, would for some time to come retain their basic importance in determining the outcome of hostilities. Army General I. G. Pavlovsky, U.S.S.R. deputy minister of defense, expressed a similar view in the November issue of the magazine *Sovetsky Voin.* The emergence of Strategic Rocket Forces, according to Pavlovsky, "does not diminish the role of the ground troops. As formerly, they remain an important branch of the armed forces." The post-Khrushchev line of all-around development of military striking power was further boosted by Admiral V. A. Kasatonov, a former member of Stalin's general staff who, in June 1965, won promotion and was now first deputy chief of naval forces. Kasatonov declared that the Soviet Navy had "colossal strategic-operational capabilities" and "for the first time in its history the Navy has been transformed in the fullest sense into a long-range offensive arm of the armed forces." The intensive building of helicopter carriers, KRESTA-class cruisers with guided missiles, destroyers and submarines, and the training of naval infantry under Army auspices were prominent aspects of contemporary military activity.

The Air Force, too, was rapidly undergoing expansion and modernization. By 1968 it was reported by the Institute for Strategic Studies to have 750 medium bombers, 200 heavy bombers, 4000 tactical aircraft, 1500 helicopters and 1500 air transports, with many new, long-range ANTONOV 22s.

A sizable increase in the output of military and space hardware was implied by the large rise in defense expenditure authorized at the meeting of the Supreme Soviet in October 1967. According to the U.S. secretary of defense, the U.S.S.R. increased its arsenal of ICBMs from 720 to about 1000 by April 1969, and more than doubled its force of long-range, submarine-launched missiles. By the end of 1978, the Soviet totals are expected to reach 1290 ICBMs and 300 submarine-launched missiles, according to the U.S. president's report of February 18, 1970. These giant strides forward in the realm of armaments required the creation of new defense ministries. In February 1968, an All-Union Ministry of the Machine Building Industry was established under V. Bakhirev, formerly of the Ministry of Defense Industry. The new ministry was thought to be engaged in the manufacture of guns or rockets or possibly tracked vehicles. A leitmotif of party propaganda organized around the 50th anniversary of the Red Army was preparation of the armed forces to conduct combat operations "with both conventional and rocket-nuclear weapons." During this recent anniversary Admiral S. G. Gorshkov, commander-in-chief of the Soviet Navy, stated that the Soviet Navy had become "an instrument of strategic activity," and the Commander of the Leningrad Naval Academy, Rear Admiral Khrenov, said that the Soviet fleet was being transformed from a coastal into an oceanic force. On December 25, 1968, Major General Ye. Silimov declared in *Red Star* that the party adhered to "the principle of the priority or first-call of defense needs."

IV.

Changing Modes of Destalinization

The selective rehabilitation of Stalin, a prominent feature of the increasingly vocal influence of the Soviet military after the spring of 1965, was paralleled in other sectors of Soviet life as well, particularly in ideology, the arts, sciences, and culture. The post-Khrushchev regime moved slowly and for about six months destalinization seemed to be continuing, but at a slower pace. Some of Khrushchev's eccentric policies were reversed, and a more tolerant attitude seemed to prevail towards research in genetics, sociology, social psychology, cybernetics, and statistics. Victims of Stalin's purges continued to be rehabilitated.

Beginning in April and May, 1965, these trends were slowed down, halted, and in some cases reversed. A general crackdown on intellectual and artistic freedom was initiated, and excessive criticism of the "cult of personality" was sharply condemned. Ideological lines hardened and dissenting intellectuals were crudely threatened. This wave of repression culminated in the arrest of the writers Andrei Sinyavsky and Yuli Daniel in September 1965, on charges of conducting "anti-Soviet agitation and propaganda." Alexei Rumiantsev, editor-in-chief of *Pravda,* and defender of liberal writers, was replaced in September by an old party functionary, Mikhail Zimyanin, who was retrieved from the Foreign Ministry to which he had been exiled by Khrushchev. Sergei Trapeznikov, a veteran ideological "dogmatist," who was placed in charge of science and education under Party Secretary Demichev, published an important article in *Pravda* on October 8, 1965, condemning historians, "pseudo-theoreticians," and others who were excessively preoccupied with the negative aspects of the Stalin era.

Tension mounted as Sinyavsky and Daniel were sentenced to long terms of imprisonment on February 14, 1966. Valery Tarsis, another outspoken writer, had his citizenship revoked "for action discreditable to a citizen of the U.S.S.R." A number of lesser-known authors and critics were in the meantime taken into custody for protesting the resort to police-state methods. It is scarcely coincidental that in January 1966 *Pravda* denounced as "wrong and non-Marxian" the anti-Stalin term "cult of the individual" and urged historians to portray the Stalin era more positively. In February the same newspaper heartily praised A. A. Zhdanov, leader of the postwar tightening of ideological discipline and organizer of the Cominform, on the 70th anniversary of his birth.

These events and trends provoked fear and consternation among Soviet scientists, intellecuals, and artists. A general atmosphere of anxiety and apprehension enveloped Soviet life. Many citizens, some only recently released from Soviet prisons and camps, were fearful that Stalinism was about to return.

These fears generated rumors that Stalin's complete rehabilitation was to take place at the 23rd Party Congress, to be held from March 29 to April 8, 1966. In protest, a petition was sent to the Central Committee signed by 27 prominent Soviet intellectuals, scientists, and artists. Communist leaders in Italy and elsewhere also registered objections and it is very likely that powerful voices within the Soviet Presidium also dissented.

Neither Stalin nor Stalinism was rehabilitated at the Congress. Nevertheless continuity with many aspects of the Stalinist past was restored in a low-keyed manner at the Congress. The Presidium of the Central Committee was renamed Politburo, as it was called during the greater part of Stalin's rule. The post of First Party Secretary, occupied by Brezhnev since October 1964, was henceforth to be known as General Secretary, that is, the title used by Stalin at the height of his career. New curbs on party membership were decreed in the vein of a lately resurrected statement that, "Our party is a fortress whose doors open only to those who have been verified." The restrictions in effect denoted the scrapping of Khrushchev's concept of the C.P.S.U. as a "party of the whole people." Moreover, the stage was set for a revival of political purges with an edict that "the party shall rid itself of individuals who violate the C.P.S.U. Program and Rules and compromise the high title of Communist by their conduct." The procedures for appealing party punishment were accordingly made more difficult. The traditional barrier standing between party and non-party members was raised once more by dint of excluding the possibility of Khrushchev-type Central Committee meetings attended by thousands of ordinary workers and farmers. Bureaucratic privilege was also safeguarded through the repeal of Khrushchev's order providing for the rotation of party executive officers.

Critics of Stalin's iron rule and essential thought were severely lectured at the 23rd Congress. N. G. Yegorychev, first secretary of the Moscow City Party Committee, berated those who would "seek out in the country's political life some elements of so-called 'Stalinism' as a bogey-man to frighten society and especially the intelligentsia." Yegorychev opposed "any attempts to write off the heroic history of our people who, under the party's leadership, traveled the difficult but glorious path of struggle and triumphs for almost a half-century." General Yepishev pointed up "the glorious fighting and revolutionary traditions of the older generation." He indicated that Stalinist military doctrine with its appreciation of the requirements of non-nuclear warfare was not hopelessly outdated: "Under the pretense of an 'innovative' approach to the development of theory there are sometimes attempts to subject to doubt the basic views of the classics of Marxism-Leninism on the common laws governing military affairs." The veteran diplomat I. M. Maisky, who had a reputation for pro-Western sympathies and was a signatory of the petition imploring the Soviet leaders not to rehabilitate Stalin, was attacked by Georgian party secretary and Presidium candidate member V. P. Mzhavanadze on grounds of falsifying history in his anti-Stalin memoirs of the Second World War. All this was fitting prelude to the upgrading of Stalin in party literature to the exalted position of a "big Marxist theoretician" and "disciple of Lenin."

The gradual and selective rehabilitation of Stalin continued through 1966. On January 7, 1967, in a major Central Committee decree ushering in the 50th jubilee year of the Soviet State,

Stalin's crimes were dismissed as mere "temporary setbacks and mistakes." And the 25,000-word "Theses" on the 50th anniversary of the Bolshevik Revolution warmly praised the wisdom of Stalin's program of military industrialization in the 1930s and his wartime leadership. Only brief mention was made of the terroristic excesses under Stalin, and these were again brushed off as "temporary setbacks and errors." The "Theses" strongly affirmed the virtues of military preparedness and social discipline. Khrushchev's "state of the entire people"—a doctrinal formula intended to reconcile party and popular interests—was said to be a continuation of the Lenin-Stalin "dictatorship of the proletariat." The Soviet Union and other socialist states were dedicated to the waging of "class-struggle against imperialism in the international arena." The recurrent themes of this latest ideological treatise of Soviet Communism were the continuity of policy and infallibility of party leadership. It was in this atmosphere that Professor A. N. Nekrich, author of the book *June 22, 1941,* which debunked the Hitler-Stalin nonaggression pact, was expelled from membership in the Soviet Communist Party.

V.

The Stalin Issue in Perspective

It should come as no surprise that the resurgence of the military-industrial-apparatus complex in the Soviet leadership and the progressive squelching of intellectual and artistic dissent in the face of increasingly conservative-oriented policies has encouraged the secret police to stage a marked recovery. The increasing emphasis on national security and ideological conformity could not help but revive the morale of police officials, since once again they would be called upon to perform "patriotic" services for the country. And yet, of course, the revival of the police as a powerful socio-institutional force could not but simultaneously arouse both the suspicion and fears of the traditional military. They seem to share an interest with conservative party functionaries in ideological conformity but not in reviving the police as the institutional mechanism of control. As long as the professional military look with concern and apprehension on the possible rise of the K.G.B. to anything approaching its former significance, it is likely that the military can thwart a return to a full-scale police state.

Nevertheless, beginning with Police Chief Vladimir Semichastny's article in *Pravda* of May 7, 1955, praising the traditions and work of the *Cheka,* while glossing over the crimes of the Stalin era, a definite attempt was made to refurbish the image of the police. The publicity campaign that followed, including the glorification of Soviet secret agent Colonel Rudolf Abel, apparently backfired.

Other members of the Soviet leadership probably looked askance at the attempt of the young and ambitious Shelepin (Semichastny's predecessor and mentor) to improve and consolidate his position within the conservative coalition and thus within the leadership as a whole. After Khrushchev's ouster, no member of the Soviet leadership held as many overlapping institutional positions in the Soviet hierarchy. Shelepin was the only leader with simultaneous membership in the Presidium, Secretariat and Presidium of the Council of Ministers (as a deputy premier). In addition, he was chairman of the Committee for Party and State Control, and his protégé, Semichastny, was in charge of the K.G.B.

Shelepin's threat to the other members of the Soviet leadership appeared so ominous that in 1965, he was forced to relinquish his position as deputy premier and chairman of the Committee on Party and State Control, which was then dissolved. He remained, however, a member of the Presidium and Secretariat, but was no longer in charge of a state administrative agency. His power and authority were further diminished in 1967 when he was shifted out of the Secretariat and into the less imposing job of chairman of the Trade Union Council. In addition, his crony, Semichastny was deprived of his position as Chief of the K.G.B. by Uri Andropov in May 1967 and downgraded to the post of first deputy chairman of the Ukranian Council of Ministers. The following month, Yegorychev, who appears to have been connected with Shelepin, was deprived of his key post in the Moscow party organization.

There can be little question that the hardening of ideological controls and the intimidation of dissenting intellectuals gives greater prominence to police activities. But Stalin's rehabilitation, the process of restalinization and the resurrection of stalinism are complex questions that must be placed in proper perspective. The issue of Stalin's rehabilitation as a historical figure and political personality must be sharply distinguished from the revival of his methods and policies. Since Stalin is still a gruesome memory to millions of living Russians, the two have a tendency to become intertwined. Any attempt to place Stalin in objective, historical perspective is bound to arouse apprehensions that the leadership, or parts of it, are subjectively predisposed to the resurrection of Stalinist ideological and political norms. And yet, aside from the fact that the rehabilitation of Stalin will affect the political fortunes of various individuals and groups unevenly, Stalin must be extricated from the morass of tendentious distortions and self-serving falsehoods generated by Khrushchev and his followers, if Soviet history, ideology, and policy is to proceed from positions of relative objectivity, rather than from opposing images of falsification. Just as some Soviet leaders and citizens may have a vested interest in preserving Stalinist falsifications and distortions, some Soviet citizens seem to have developed a self-interest in preserving intact Khrushchev's distortions and falsifications about Stalin, but not those concerning Khrushchev.

A close reading of the Soviet press reveals many positions on the Stalin issue. There are some who would like simply to forget Stalin and his crimes; others would ignore only his crimes, while still others say that he committed no crimes at all, but "errors" and "mistakes;" and there are still others who consider Stalin's "crimes" not as crimes, but as virtues. On the other hand, we find views that are uncompromising in their condemnation and denunciation of everything connected with Stalin; still others that wish to preserve the distortions and falsifications of the Khrushchev era; and there are those that demand an intensified search for more "crimes" of the Stalin era, and rehabilitation of more victims. Between these extremes there are those who claim to strive for "balanced" appraisals of the entire Stalin period, including accounts that deal with his policies and actions on a strictly ad hoc basis, i.e., judging each policy and action separately on its merits. It should be noted that the decisions of the 20th and 22nd Congresses dealing with Stalin and the cult of personality have been reaffirmed but not celebrated.

On balance, however, the number of articles and statements designed to mitigate, nullify, or gloss over the condemnations of Stalin outweigh those that reaffirm the entire Khrushchev destalinization process.

It is these conflicting cross-currents concerning Stalin that convey the appearance of a seesaw battle between Stalin's proponents and detractors. Actually, diverse views continue to be expressed, with varying degrees of intensity and official blessing, in accordance with the complex, fluctuating factional conflicts in the leadership. Stalin continues to be simultaneously praised, damned, and ignored, and the revival of "positive" views concerning him can be considered as much a relaxation of previous restrictions as a threat to his detractors. Under Khrushchev, an objective appraisal of Stalin, to say nothing of outright praise, was severely circumscribed and officially frowned upon. The selective rehabilitation of Stalin must, therefore, be seen in this context rather than in the context of the revival of Stalinism. During the Khrushchev decade, the charge of "Stalinist" or "Stalinism" was often loosely applied to Soviet conservatives, more in face-to-face confrontations than in print, and it became a useful weapon in the arsenal of the "liberalizers" in their battle with the "dogmatists."

During the first months of 1968, the controversy over Stalin revealed itself in limited yet graphic terms. In February, *Kommunist* published an article entitled, "For Leninist Party Spirit in the Interpretation of the History of the CPSU," by V. Golikov, S. Murashev, I. Chkhikvishili, N. Shatagin and C. Shaumyan. The article was an undisguised attempt to mitigate and even whitewash some aspects of the Stalinist era by arguing that the party's strictures on the "cult of personality" should be limited and defined by the Central Committee resolution of June 30, 1956, which was a relatively pallid and abstract criticism of the Stalin era. The authors of the article apparently would choose to ignore both Khrushchev's secret speech at the 20th Party Congress and the resolutions of the 22nd Party Congress, expelling Stalin's corpse from Lenin's tomb. This article stakes out one end of the spectrum of opinion on the Stalin issue.

The other pole of the spectrum is not likely to find outlets in the Soviet media. This position vigorously attacks Stalin and calls for intensification of the destalinization program, condemnation of Stalin and his methods, and rehabilitation of virtually all of the political personalities who opposed him. These views are often mimeographed and circulated privately. Some are smuggled abroad where they are published. The extraordinary memorandum written by the prominent Soviet physicist Andrei Sakharov falls into this category, as does a similar document by Leonid Petrovsky, a concentration camp veteran and grandson of Greg Petrovsky, an "old Bolshevik" incarcerated by Stalin. In April 1969, Petrovsky sent an open letter to the Central Committee and the magazine

Kommunist (which refused to print it), denouncing the four authors of the article mentioned above, and offering its publication as evidence that "even today guarantees against tyranny are lacking." The author, who has since been expelled from the party, calls for a continuation and intensification of the denunciation of Stalin and attacks some members of the current leadership by implication. The author villifies almost everything connected with Stalin and calls for the rehabilitation of practically all of Stalin's political opponents, including, among others, Bukharin, Rykov, Tomsky, Kamenev, Zinoviev, and Piatakov. Apparently only Trotsky, Yagoda, and Yezhov would remain to share oblivion with Stalin.

A so-called balanced view prevailing at the summit was reflected in an article appearing in the February 1969 issue of *The World Marxist Review* by Boris Ponomaryov, a member of the Secretariat and leading Soviet ideologist associated with conservative positions. It mentions Stalin twice—once, favorably in passing in conjunction with other people, and once, unfavorably, as follows:

> The C.P.S.U. Comintern delegation—Stalin, Zhdanov, Manuilsky, Knorin, Piatnitsky, Gusev and others—played a big part in the fight against the Trotskyites and Right opportunists for a correct Comintern policy. (p. 14.)

> Unfortunately, the adverse consequences of the Stalin personality cult, accompanied as it was by a departure from Leninist norms, had their effect also on the Comintern, chiefly with regard to its cadres. It will be recalled that the C.P.S.U. resolutely condemned all manifestations of the personality cult at its 20th and subsequent congresses, and took measures to eliminate its consequences. (p. 16.)

On March 26, 1969, Mikhail Suslov, a member of both the Politburo and the Secretariat and a veteran ideologist often characterized as a "Stalinist," reaffirmed Ponomarev's position in a speech marking the 50th anniversary of the Comintern. He stated that "unfortunately the consequences of the cult of Stalin adversely affected the activity of the Comintern in its later years."

Destalinization continues in certain important respects. To be sure, there is greater repression of intellectual and artistic freedom, but only because there is greater opportunity for the expression of dissent and opposition. The suppression of dissent, which is characteristic of the current period, must be distinguished from the prevention of dissent, which was a characteristic feature of Stalin's day. Dissent and opposition continue to manifest themselves in Soviet society. Indeed one might say that more of it exists under the Brezhnev-Kosygin regime than under Khrushchev, if for no other reason than that many of the current dissenters were Khrushchev partisans and, therefore, had little or no reason to dissent.

Though the ideological balance has tipped over to the conservatives, Stalin's corpse still lies in its shabby, uncelebrated grave, surrounded by weeds and wilted flowers, behind Lenin's imposing tomb. This is perhaps the most eloquent and symbolic reflection of Stalin's place in Soviet life today.

The complex trends were further continued in the revised *History of the C.P.S.U.*, published in late 1969. Although produced by the identical board of editors (chaired by B. V. Ponamarev) that presided over the publication of the 1962 Khrushchevite edition, the new version betrays a considerable departure from the old in its treatment of Stalin and the "cult of personality." It should be noted, however, that the 1962 edition appeared shortly after the 22nd Party Congress, when Stalin's corpse was banished from Lenin's mausoleum and virtually all of the current leadership engaged in an orgy of Stalin denunciation. The revised version in some respects, therefore, represents a conscious attempt to retreat from a position that may have been politically useful for Khrushchev but is increasingly counter-productive for his successors.

In the 1969 edition, the catalog of Stalin's "crimes" has been severely trimmed. Many are omitted and others reduced to "mistakes" and "errors." Thus, the section on collectivization was thoroughly revised to mute the atmosphere of terror that accompanied the entire process; more crimes are ascribed to Beria while Stalin's culpability is correspondingly diminished. The hints in the earlier edition that Stalin was somehow implicated in Kirov's assassination have been dropped, as was an earlier assertion that Stalin used Kirov's death "to begin dealing with people summarily who did not agree with him . . . [which] was the beginning of wholesale repressive measures and most flagrant violations of socialist legality."

References to the "cult of personality," a phrase that appears to have increasingly outlived its utility since 1966, seem to have been singled out for deletion. Similarly, the extensive inventory of Stalin's character defects has been pruned, while earlier allusions to Stalin's opposition to Lenin in 1909, 1917, and 1918 are dropped. All of this falls short of rehabilitation, but nevertheless constitutes a substantial refurbishment that requires explanation.

VI.

Why Restalinization?

Destalinization reached its zenith around the time of the 22nd Party Congress in October, 1961. Soon thereafter it leveled off and then was arrested gradually and in some isolated instances even reversed. The leveling off process continued under Khrushchev's successors, but in late 1965 a reverse current began. It emerged to compete with the residual pressures for continuing the destalinization process, which in some cases, as noted earlier, was moving beyond mere destalinization. By the time of the 23rd Party Congress in April 1966, the pressures exerted in the direction of rehabilitating Stalin had gathered considerable momentum, and have continued at a moderately accelerated pace, though in an erratic and selective fashion.

The selective though unmistakable and accelerating rehabilitation of Stalin since Khrushchev's ouster represents complex and contradictory currents in both the Soviet leadership and the elite structure of Soviet society. The rehabilitation of Stalin involves both symbolic and substantive issues, for it is at once obvious that the revival of Stalin as a historical personage is a prerequisite, but not necessarily a prelude, to the revival of what is characterized as "Stalinism." Stalin's rehabilitation as a person need not necessarily require the restoration of Stalin as a charismatic symbol.

The revival of Stalin as a person and Stalinism as a system affects different individuals, political factions, institutions, social groups, nationalities, and generations unevenly, and in a manner that produces not simple polarization, but a discrete fracturing of positions. These positions can be loosely plotted along both a horizontal axis, representing various issues at different points along the axis (i.e., Stalin's role as wartime commander-in-chief, collectivization, ideological controls, heavy industry, the purges, etc.), and along a vertical axis representing a continuum of sentiment ranging from absolute opposition to near total revival of Stalinist norms. This allows for a bewildering array of positions that often appear confusing and contradictory.

Why is Stalin being rehabilitated? What purposes are being served by his rehabilitation? Who is supporting his rehabilitation? Who opposes? Who benefits and who loses from his rehabilitation?

Some rehabilitation of Stalin was inevitable at a particular point in time, not only to do justice to the historical record, but because Stalin was the principal architect of the state founded by Lenin, and is irrevocably connected with the Soviet system. No amount of tampering with history could break this link. The continued consignment of Stalin to oblivion, to say nothing of perpetuating his denunciation, threatened to erode and undermine the basic legitimacy of the Soviet system. And while the initial denunciation of Stalin was functionally necessary in order to reform and adapt the frozen Soviet monolith to changing social reality, it had become emphatically clear by about 1963 that the continued denunciation of Stalin was proving to be counter-productive for the Soviet leadership and large segments of the Soviet elite.

Thus, in order to place the restalinization phenomenon in the proper context, it is necessary to examine the actual and threatened consequences of the destalinization policy as perceived by the Soviet leadership as a whole, as well as by its constituent factional and institutional sectors. These can be summarized as follows:

Anti-Sovietism as anti-Stalinism

The denunciation of Stalin in 1956 and Khrushchev's policy of destalinization provided not only a haven for those who wished to strengthen and revitalize the Soviet system through reform, adaptation, and liberalization, but also inadvertently unleashed critics of the Soviet system who donned the guise of anti-Stalinists. The emptying of the concentration camps released thousands of inmates who were bitter not only toward Stalin but toward the regime that unjustly incarcerated them. From this group came the concentration camp literature.

The most famous and significant novel was Solzhenitsyn's *One Day in the Life of Ivan Denisovich*. Solzhenitsyn typifies, in the mind of the Soviet leadership, the bitter, irredeemable anti-Soviet critic. Few among the thousands of ex-concentration camp inmates have the special talents of a Solzhenitsyn with which to vent their vengeance. Nevertheless, covert and latent forms of anti-Sovietism flourish in the writings of secretly disaffected "internal emigres" among the creative intelligentsia. Their writings "for the drawer", are often circulated privately, or smuggled out of the country to be published under pseudonyms (Daniel and Sinyavsky) or "without their permission" (Pasternak, Eugenia Ginzberg, etc.). Other writers skirted the margins of anti-Sovietism (Yevtushenko, Voznesensky, Kuznetsov, Tvardovsky, *et. al.*) during the heyday of Khrushchev's "liberalization."

Destalinization thus threatened to develop its own inner dynamic among the creative Soviet intelligentsia and metamorphose into various forms of anti-Sovietism that could become endemic among intellectual, academic, and scientific circles and eventually infect the Soviet public as a whole.

The Stalinist generation

The overwhelming majority of Soviet bureaucrats, functionaries, professionals, and technicians in the Soviet system were reared and indoctrinated in the Stalinist tradition. Many of them benefited from the Stalinist terror, which gave them career opportunities at an early age. Most had accommodated themselves to Stalinist standards, practices, and institutions. Their personal positions prompted continued defense and support of the system.

The denunciation of Stalin and his methods thus served to tarnish an entire generation of strategically placed functionaries. They became vulnerable targets not only of the "liberalizers" and "reformers," but of ambitious subordinates, embittered employees, alienated relatives (including their own children), ordinary citizens with personal scores, and above all, purge victims and their relatives. Many of these officials, particularly those in the Soviet police and the party apparatus, were implicated in the repressive actions of the Stalinist era and were thus considered fair game by both anti-Stalinist and anti-Soviet elements. As a consequence, not only demoralization, but functional incapacitation set in as various middle-ranking officials were branded as "little Stalins" by Khrushchev "reformers." This demoralization appeared in all structures and institutions, but with particular virulence in the party apparatus, industrial bureaucracy, state and collective farms, and the state bureaucracy. Conservative intellectuals and scientists were attacked by liberals, and even the armed forces came in for criticism and condemnation as quasi-pacifist sentiments cropped up in various journals and magazines.

Disorientation of Soviet Youth

The condemnation of Stalin, continued destalinization, and constant criticism and attacks upon the system threatened to create the Soviet version of the "generation gap," which exists to some degree in any event. Dissent and criticism of the regime became fashionable among students at major centers of higher education as young people more and more took their cue from anti-Stalinists, "liberalizers," "reformers," and folk heroes, like Yevtushenko, whom they wished to emulate. This hampered the proper socialization of the younger generation, who, in the eyes of the Soviet leadership, were not sufficiently mature and experienced to discriminate between "negative" and "positive" aspects of the long Stalinist era. Under the impact of destalinization, idealistic Soviet youth questioned the enormous gap between communist doctrine and practice, between the system's promises and its achievements, and demanded that the constitutional guarantees of free speech and free press be practiced. In the absence of authoritative interpretations of Marxism-Leninism, various manifestations of youthful "revisionism" took shape in response to the ideological vacuum created by the repudiation of Stalinist formulations. Students questioned and challenged their professors and issued "wall newspapers." They criticized various polices of the regime and rejected official explanations and rationalizations offered by their professors, administrators, and party officials. Enthusiasm for the Komsomol rapidly deteriorated and in some instances Komsomol organizations were converted into vehicles of dissent and criticism.

Erosion of the System

The denunciation of Stalin and the repudiation of Stalinism not only eroded the legitimacy of the Soviet leadership of the world communist movement and undermined Soviet control of Eastern Europe, but also threatened to undermine the legitimacy of the Soviet system in Russia itself. The disaffection of the intelligentsia, the demoralization of the bureaucrats and the threatened alienation of youth, all served to subvert the basic foundations of the Soviet social and political order. Destalinization thus threatened to unstabilize the Soviet system itself since both Stalin's methods and institutions were called into question. Almost all existing Soviet institutions were created by Stalin and inherited by his successors virtually intact. The Soviet Constitution itself is the personal handiwork of Stalin and is universally known as the "Stalin Constitution." Because of Stalin's identification with the constitution, Khrushchev planned to replace it with one of his own. Apparently, this plan has been shelved, if not scrapped entirely. Disentangling Stalin and Stalinism from the Soviet system proved to be an insuperable task, since the two are virtuallly identical. The one-party system, the Soviet electoral system and legislative process, the federal structure, and the administrative complex are all not only Stalinist in inspiration and design, but have become eternally Soviet as well. Thus, destalinization threatened to unravel the entire social order: collectivization; the three-class social order; the system of incentives and rewards; and the delicate system of national autonomy, all of which are integral parts of the Stalinist legacy. Hence, the post-Khrushchev leadership may feel that the most prudent way to arrest further destalinization and repair the damage done to the legitimacy of the Soviet system is to restore, at least in part, the legitimacy of the Stalin era.

Destalinization in Foreign Policies

Although Soviet doctrine defines foreign policy as an extension of domestic policy, not even Khrushchev dared to attack directly Stalin's conduct of Soviet affairs. To be sure, while certain doctrines and foreign policy positions inescapably associated with Stalin were renounced or modified, no overt attacks were ever made or tolerated. The renunciation of territorial demands upon Turkey, the reconciliation with Tito, the unilateral renunciation of bases in Finland, the relinquishment of Soviet rights in China, the Austrian State Treaty and the normalization of relations with Japan were among the principal departures from the course set by Stalin. Although Khrushchev declared Stalin suspicious, vicious in character, and bordering on insanity in his internal policies, none of this was supposed to have affected his relations with the outside world. In his relations with foreign states, Stalin was presumably in full possession of his faculties, and motivated only by the highest ideals of communism. But dark episodes of Stalin's foreign policy were always available for re-examination, possible criticism, and condemnation. These included Stalin's miscalculation of Hitler's rise, the Nazi-Soviet Pact of 1939, and Hitler-Stalin collaboration thereafter. It would almost certainly include Stalin's postwar attitude towards the United States and his involvement in the initiation of the Korean War. Stalin's mistakes in policy toward communist Eastern Europe were conveniently foisted upon Beria, although the dictator did not escape completely unscathed. Questioning Stalin's domestic policy created problems enough, as did criticism of his relations with communist countries, but to allow his foreign policies towards the capitalist world to be placed in doubt would raise problems beyond Soviet control that could have ominous implications.

The partial rehabilitation of Stalin, when viewed against these actual and threatened consequences of his denunciation, emerges as essentially defensive in character and largely designed for achieving domestic objectives. The rehabilitation process does have some prophylactic purposes where foreign policy is concerned, but its impact is largely indirect. It would be a mistake to assume a priori that restalinization at home and in Eastern Europe will necessarily lead to a more belligerent or aggressive foreign policy. On the contrary, as will be explained below, a tightening of the screws at home may be necessary to protect Soviet society from the feedback effects of a possible détente with the noncommunist world and relaxation of international tensions.

The Soviet social system, as it exists today, still betrays a deplorably low threshold of tolerance for the social vibrations that can be set in motion if the Soviet populace is confronted with an alternative set of policy options that might prove to be more attractive than the choices of the regime in power. To be sure, Khrushchev deliberately excited social vibrations because he wanted to fashion new, broader social and power constituencies to challenge his rivals who cultivated the older, socially narrower, and more conservative constituencies upon which he himself had relied earlier against Malenkov and the "anti-party group." It is precisely because of this that the dominant conservative coalition in the current Soviet leadership is determined to severely limit dissent and criticism.

Stalinism and Stalin are relevant in this connection because some of the policies adopted in recent years are closely associated in the minds of the people with Stalin, namely continued priority—at a lower level to be sure—of heavy industry and military preparedness. Thus, an article in *Krasnaya Zvezda* (September 25, 1969), without actually mentioning Stalin, in effect strongly endorsed the Stalinist emphasis on the inherent interdependence of heavy industry and national defense, by ascribing the policy to Lenin. "V. I. Lenin regarded heavy industry as the fundamental basis of military might, of a country's defense capability," the article states and then goes on to show that the application of this principle (by Stalin, of course, although not mentioned) enabled the Soviet Union to win the war against Nazi Germany and attain its existing military power. Criticism of Stalin tends to tarnish policies associated with him, so if such criticism can be silenced, the factional critics of existing policy are deprived of a useful surrogate target.

Silencing the critics of Stalin also serves to stabilize the system by strengthening those who are its supporters and defenders. In the first place, it raises the morale and efficiency of the sizable army of middle-aged, middle-ranking bureaucrats, who were often the specific targets of the anti-Stalinists. Since these bureaucrats are generously distributed in the party apparatus, the heavy industrial bureaucracy and the armed forces, the strengthening of their position reinforces those institutions that are already predisposed to conservative positions. It also improves the relative position of conservative forces in other institutions where the "liberalizers" and "reformers" are apt to be concentrated (the creative intelligentsia, light and consumer goods industry, education, science, etc.). All this, in turn, further supports the power and authority of the conservative factions at the political summit.

The principal areas of restalinization in the broadest sense are three in number and seem to correspond with the interests of the most conservative and stability-oriented structures in the Soviet system. These are:

Controls on Arts and Sciences

The most directly and conspicuously visible targets of restalinization are the intellectuals. Their dissent and criticism can become an independent source of values, norms and goals in opposition to those generated and propagated by the party apparatus and its ideologues. Restoration of Stalinist-type ideological controls thus serves to repress the creation of competing values and at the same time preserves the power and social function of the party apparatus.

Priority of Heavy Industry

One of the chief beneficiaries of Stalin's rehabilitation has been heavy industry. This is not because it constitutes a distinctive power structure in its own right, but largely because it is highly valued by both the party apparatus and the traditional military. When one speaks of the priority of heavy industry, it should be made quite clear that this does not in any way imply the restoration of its previous overwhelming priority, but rather continuation of priority at a lower level and more protection against the erosion of its budgetary allocations. The recentralization of the economic ministries after Khrushchev's ouster served to strengthen heavy industry's position.

Military Rehabilitation of Stalin's Record

Although the armed forces suffered terribly at the hands of Stalin, the damage was chiefly to individuals rather than institutions. Institutionally, the traditional military appears to be "Stalinist" in that Stalin always emphasized a powerful military establishment (but under his undisputed control).

The military has been particularly zealous in rehabilitating Stalin's wartime leadership, apparently because criticism of Stalin's military policy tended to taint the reputation of the armed forces. Critics implied that Stalin's military commanders were either incompetent for having given Stalin bad advice or that they were too cowardly and craven to dispute Stalin's disastrous military decisions. The rehabilitation of Stalin as wartime commander serves to silence the critics of the military's complicity in the disasters of World War II.

The relaxation of ideological controls in the arts enabled quasi-pacifists and anti-militarists to condemn war, criticize the military as a career, question military victory as a fount of patriotism, and generally portray the military in a bad light. Marshals and generals openly complained that this literature was seriously undermining the morale and effectiveness of the armed forces. There is, thus, a coincidence of interests with the party ideologues on this score.

The impact of Stalin's rehabilitation on Soviet relations with the outside world will be largely indirect. As the Soviet Union moves into the 1970s, it will simultaneously be confronted with an increasingly belligerent China armed with thermonuclear warheads and missiles. As U.S. involvement in East Asia and Southeast Asia is wound down, there will probably be a resurgence of Japanese power and influence in East Asia to contend with as well. In the west, while Moscow's occupation of Czechoslovakia has temporarily stabilized Soviet power in Eastern Europe, the economic strength and political aspirations of West Germany will continue to pose a challenge to Soviet influence in the area. And finally, the Soviet Union will continue to compete with the U.S. on a global scale in various parts of the world.

All of this means that the Soviet leadership must be assured of an ideologically disciplined, psychologically attuned, and rapidly responsive population. The psychological pliability of the Soviet population becomes even more critical in the face of a fragmented leadership. Thus, the Soviet population must be so disciplined and conditioned that it can respond to rapid changes in policy. To the degree that criticism and dissent is tolerated, then to that degree will the Soviet public be less amenable to manipulation. To the degree that the continued denunciation of Stalin is permitted, then to that degree will the faith of the Soviet public in the system and its leadership erode.

It appears quite possible that, if the Soviet leaders reach or negotiate a détente with the United States, the Kremlin may wish to control or minimize the internal impact that a relaxation of international tensions may have in dulling the vigilance of the general populace and encouraging the disruptive impulses of the intelligentsia. The rehabilitation of Stalin thus serves to dampen both these tendencies. Moreover it may be desired to be better able to deal with a menacing China, or to exploit quickly any advantage or opportunity that might develop, and also to maintain a given social and factional equilibrium at home and discourage the resurrection of a threat from the west in the event of difficulties in Eastern Europe or elsewhere.

One final defensive intent of the rehabilitation of Stalin as it affects foreign policy:

It is quite evident that the regime is opposed to any critical re-examination of Stalin's foreign policy that might result from an exuberant anti-Stalinism. While the Soviet leaders might be able to handle the effects of destalinization at home, a reappraisal of Stalin's foreign policy might create problems outside the purview of Soviet control or influence. Territorial issues are a case in point. As the principal beneficiary of 250,000 square miles of territorial annexations in Europe and Asia, the Soviet Union is peculiarly vulnerable. Should any of these annexations be questioned by Soviet critics or historians, it could only serve to legitimize the latent and overt demands for territorial restitution by at least six bordering countries. It is mainly for this reason that Soviet historians cannot publicly scrutinize and discuss the era of Nazi-Soviet collaboration, although they deal with the problem privately in their meetings and discussions. The entire outside world is privy to the details of the secret protocols, arrangements, and negotiations that transpired between Moscow and Berlin from April, 1939, to June, 1941, relating to the denunciation of spheres of influence and territorial dismemberment of adjoining states. Soviet historians, however, cannot admit their existence, for to admit their existence would be to negate the legitimacy of the territorial transfers.

VII.

The Contemporary Crisis in Foreign Policy

Some of the trends and tendencies of Khrushchev's foreign policy mobilized distinct constituencies and assumed a certain autonomous momentum of their own with which his successors must contend. These became, in effect, conditioning factors that continue to shape Soviet international policies. The factors can be summarized as follows: (1) The erosion of ideology resulting in a loss of overall purpose and direction in foreign policy; (2) the fragmentation of the decision-making process which contributes a cycle of further erosion of ideology and more leadership fragmentation; (3) the globalization of Soviet foreign policy, which has extended the scope and range of Soviet commitments in world affairs at a time of diminishing purpose and fragmenting will; and (4) the relative growth in Soviet military capabilities.

The Khrushchev Legacy

The contemporary crisis in Soviet foreign policy thus can be defined as a divided leadership confronted with expanding obligations and increasing military power, but lacking a unity of purpose. This serves to create instability, unpredictability in behavior, and diminished capability for the rational control and containment of dangerous situations. Not only the Czech occupation in 1968, but also the Arab-Israeli War the year before, served to bring these contradictory currents in the Soviet leadership clearly into view. Soviet policy in both instances seemed to veer from one extreme to another.

The conditioning factors described above, individually as well as in dynamic interaction, have impact on future trends in Soviet foreign policy. If Soviet foreign policy were to progressively abandon Marxist-Leninist ideology, it might be expected that conflict and violence would lose appeal as sources of political and diplomatic gain. But such a trend could have just the opposite effect by inciting the Soviet state to behave more in the fashion of a traditional imperialist power, according to its role in world affairs and the momentum of its power. Ideologically calculated use of violence to promote world communism may thus be supplanted by opportunistic, expedient resort to force to promote Soviet power and prestige, irrespective of its relevance to world communism.

Similarly, continued fragmentation of the Soviet leadership into factional groupings could create an element of fortuity and unpredictability in its behavior. This could tend to create further barriers to international collaboration and stability. Furthermore, it will perhaps place an even greater burden on external countervailing power as a restraining mechanism. Dealing with a divided oligarchy, whose deliberations remain concealed and whose fluctuating dominant coalition remains essentially anonymous, can induce irrational anxieties and provoke impulsive responses in the behavior of other powers.

On the whole, the globalization of Soviet foreign policy is a factor working in favor of international stability. Global pretensions require that the Soviet leaders transcend their parochial responsibilities to communist states and parties in order to cultivate an image of concern for the interests of a wide spectrum of states with a variety of regimes and social systems. This would tend to encourage the Soviet leadership to develop a vested interest in the virtues of prestige, sensitivity to world opinion, and appreciation of outlooks and attitudes that differ from its own. At the same time, however, it weakens Moscow's role as the leader of an ideological coalition, sacrifices the interests of communist parties, and creates openings for an ambitious China to compete for the favor of neglected communist states and parties. Moreover, global concerns also run the risk of over-extension and over-commitment that might divert scarce resources away from pressing domestic problems and thus contribute to internal unrest.

As a global power, the Soviet Union will inevitably find itself in worldwide competition with the other global power, the

United States, in areas geographically remote from its vital interests. This will increase the possibilities and risks of confrontation and force the Soviet Union to assume positions for the sake of prestige. Much of this rivalry will take place in an increasingly unstable Third World, when the Soviet Union may be drawn into assuming explicit and implicit obligations forcing it to commit its power and prestige over relatively trivial issues. Soviet commitments to the Arab states illustrate what might happen in other parts of the world. The Soviet leaders, however, have so far shown great prudence and caution in this regard by spurning a major effort in sub-Saharan Africa and Latin America. Only in the Indian subcontinent have the Soviet leaders undertaken commitments that are somewhat comparable to those of the Arab states and, in this case, the solicitude is motivated more by their preoccupation with the Chinese danger than anything else.

The Failure of Condominium

Khrushchev chose a policy of accommodation and détente with the United States in July 1963, but only after his vigorous attempt to overcome U.S. strategic superiority had failed and the world was twice brought to the brink of thermonuclear war—once over Berlin and again over Cuba. The Soviet Union found itself politically over-committed, militarily vulnerable, ideologically challenged by Peking, and financially on the verge of bankruptcy. In return for the respite gained by signing the test-ban treaty, which was a tacit recognition and acceptance of U.S. strategic superiority, Khrushchev elevated U.S.-U.S.S.R. relations to the top priority item in Soviet foreign policy, since only an understanding between the two global powers could guarantee the avoidance of thermonuclear war. In addition, Khrushchev expected a long period of international stability and Soviet-American cooperation, which he thought would strengthen his position at home and further Soviet interests abroad.

Khrushchev's détente policy assumed the final but definite contours of a Soviet-American condominium of diarchy in the international community, whereby the two super-powers would demarcate their respective areas of vital interest, define their area of common interest, delineate the status quo that was to be preserved, and establish the guidelines that would govern their competition in peripheral areas. Undoubtedly Khrushchev's concept of détente, based on a policy of Soviet-American condominium or diarchy, still holds some attraction for individual members of the current Politburo. It remained by default the basis of the Brezhnev-Kosygin foreign policy for the first two years or so, although with significant modifications.

The entire structure of Khrushchev's détente policy rested upon the assumption that the Kennedy Administration represented the sober forces in the United States and that they would continue to determine U.S. policy. Furthermore, it presupposed that Moscow and Washington shared an interest in containing German, Japanese, and Chinese revisionism. It posed, however, a serious threat to the social position, status, and general interests of the numerically small but powerful socio-functional and socio-institutional groups like the party apparatus, heavy industrial managers, and the military. Instead of conceiving and executing his détente policy so that their interests and needs might be painlessly accommodated, Khrushchev, in a bold effort to envelop and isolate his detractors, brusquely attempted to appeal directly to those broad social constituencies whose interests would be enhanced by his détente policy.

Aside from the serious internal dislocations among social priorities implied by his policies, Khrushchev's strategy and behavior also exposed the Soviet Union to new diplomatic and security vulnerabilities. This, too, contributed to a tactical area of agreement between Khrushchev's faction and his opposition. Khrushchev's policies threatened the interests of his opposition, while his behavior alienated his own faction, and his détente strategy made the Soviet Union diplomatically and militarily vulnerable. The currents merged to topple him in October 1964.

VIII.

New Departures in Foreign Policy

Both Kosygin and Brezhnev were closely associated with Khrushchev's détente policy. They subscribed to the Khrushchevite division of American leaders into "sober" and "mad" elements. Although they too were predisposed to recognize President Johnson as a representative of the former, they probably showed more concern about a possible rightward shift in the American political equilibrium. Khrushchev's ouster came hard on the heels of several events that ominously pointed towards simultaneous crises in Sino-Soviet and Soviet-American relations, which might require an entirely fresh approach in both instances. Senator Barry Goldwater's nomination for the U.S. presidency, the Tonkin Gulf retaliatory strikes, Mao's open bid for some 500,000 square miles of Soviet territory, and China's imminent explosion of an atomic bomb—all probably played a catalytic role in Khrushchev's ouster.

The displacement of Khrushchev did not at once dispel the doubts of the factional groups who were unenthusiastic about the entire détente policy. The new Brezhnev-Kosygin regime, however, could assuage the wounds and grievances of the factional opposition, particularly the military, and show greater sensitivity to their interests. Hence the pair may have been initially armed with a new consensual mandate charged with reviewing and revising existing policy if necessary. Thus, unlike Khrushchev, the new team was poised and prepared for any contingency that might develop out of the American election, ready to plug the gaps in Khrushchev's détente strategy and, if the détente policy continued, also amenable to try a new approach to Peking.

While the new leadership may have been united in its determination to retire Khrushchev, it was by no means united on its attitudes toward his external and internal policies, nor, more importantly, on the lines and direction of departure. Thus, for the next two years, the new regime embarked upon an amorphous strategy of unstructured probing in its foreign policy, seeking out soft spots and vulnerabilities in both its own policies and those of its adversaries. During this entire period, the regime systematically, but neither boisterously nor threateningly, strengthened its strategic military capabilities. It might be useful, therefore, at this point to indicate how this probing was conducted as the prelude to a discussion of developments in Sino-Soviet relations and East Europe.

Soviet Policy Hardens in the East and West

The initial statements and initiatives of the new Soviet collective leadership bearing on the conduct of foreign relations attested dissatisfaction with Khrushchev's last moves toward a further easing of east-west tensions. A visiting delegation of French communist officials was told in C.P.S.U. headquarters that in foreign policy Khrushchev had made "certain insufficiently considered policy changes." The scheduled trip of the Soviet head of government to Bonn was cancelled without explanation, and a strident propaganda campaign launched against an alleged resurgence of militarism and Nazism in West Germany. The acts of harassment and intimidation directed against the Federal Republic in 1965 included: notes to the U.S., U.K., and French embassies in Moscow (March 23); calling a planned Bundestag meeting in Berlin "provocative"; and an East German-Soviet military exercise between Berlin and the Federal Republic, obstructing the flow of overland traffiic between West Berlin and West Germany (April 3-10). A Soviet note delivered to the U.S. Embassy on April 26 protested the F.R.G.'s adoption of a law on the prosecution of Nazi war criminals. The Soviet Foreign Ministry on September 11 lodged a protest with the British ambassador regarding the training on British soil of West Germans in the handling of SERGEANT missiles capable of bearing nuclear warheads.

The public controversy with Communist China was halted and in December 1964 Khrushchev's planned meeting of pro-Soviet communist parties was postponed until March 1, 1965 "with a view to making better preparations" for a world conference. A Soviet party delegation attended the 8th Congress of the Yugoslav League of Communists, but Soviet press and radio ignored the Yugoslav leaders' praise of Khrushchev for his advocacy of "peaceful coexistence." Premier Kosygin, from February 4 to 15, 1965, traveled to the capitals of Communist China, North Vietnam and North Korea. It was later reported in the Moscow press that Kosygin outlined to Mao Tse-tung a broad program to improve Sino-Soviet relations. Kosygin, at each stop of his journey, reasserted the solidarity of the U.S.S.R. with anti-western forces. In Hanoi, he pledged the delivery of more military and economic aid in support of the revolutionary war that North Vietnam was conducting in the south. Specifically, a letter that the C.P.S.U. Central Committee sent to other communist parties early in 1966 informed them that the Soviet Union was delivering large amounts of weapons to the Democratic Republic of Vietnam, including rocket installations, anti-aircraft artillery, airplanes, tanks, coastal guns, warships, and other items. In 1965 alone, weapons and other war material worth about 500 million rubles ($550 million) were placed at the disposal of North Vietnam. Hanoi received support in the training of pilots, rocket personnel, tank drivers, artillery-men, and so on. A Soviet government statement released on February 9, during Kosygin's Asian tour and two days after U.S. air strikes in North Vietnam, warned that American "aggression" in Southeast Asia would entail a deterioration of U.S.-Soviet relations. A Soviet note of February 22 protested "provocative acts" against Soviet shipping by American military ships and planes. A statement protesting U.S. actions in Vietnam was handed to American Ambassador Foy Kohler by Soviet Foreign Minister Andrei Gromyko on March 4.

These harsh words toward the United States and conciliatory words toward China were echoed by Suslov, who delivered a secret report at the March 1965 Central Committee meeting on the consultative gathering of 19 communist parties in Moscow. The resolution based on Suslov's speech hailed "the struggle against imperialism" and attached "special importance" to the national liberation war in South Vietnam. The C.P.S.U., according to the resolution, would continue to search for an accommodation with the Chinese Communist party. And in the same year, Soviet ideological manuals degraded Khrushchev's slogan of "peaceful co-existence" from the general line of Kremlin foreign policy.

The 23rd Congress of the party, meeting in the spring of 1966, gave authoritative form to the hardening Soviet line, although by now the attempt to mend fences with Peking had failed dismally. Brezhnev, like Zhdanov at the founding session of the Cominform in 1947, delineated an unreconcilable class antagonism between peace-loving Soviet socialism and aggressive U.S. capitalism as the main feature of contemporary world politics. Brezhnev viewed peaceful coexistence as essentially "a form of class struggle between socialism and capitalism." A pledge of non-interference in the internal affairs of other states was qualified by the party chief:

> Of course, there can be no peaceful coexistence with respect to the internal processes of class and national-liberation struggle inside capitalist countries or in colonies. The principle of peaceful coexistence is inapplicable to relations between oppressors and oppressed, between colonizers and the victims of colonial oppression.

Brezhnev's listing of diplomatic priorities differed from those of Khrushchev in 1964. Khrushchev's objects of concern included the reduction of military budgets and creation of east-west control posts to avert the danger of surprise attack. Brezhnev instead showed primary interest in the questions of Vietnam and nuclear proliferation.

In his report to the Congress, Foreign Minister Gromyko reaffirmed Brezhnev's hardening line and dwelt on the imperative need to coordinate the foreign policies of the members of the "commonwealth of socialist states." His speech featured such combative terminology as "theater of struggle" in world politics and revived the Lenin-Stalin strategem of holding talks with the western powers for the purpose of exploiting differences between them. Gromyko stated explicitly that Europe held a place of "special" importance in the array of Soviet interests. The recognition of existing frontiers and elimination of the U.S. military presence on the continent were identified as basic objectives of Soviet policy.

A major ideological decree of the Central Committee issued on January 7, 1967, introducing the 50th Jubilee year of the Soviet State, escalated the rhetorical offensive closely associated with Brezhnev. It reiterated his thesis of two opposing courses locked in permanent ideological combat: "The line of peace and freedom of the peoples, embodied in socialism, and the line of war and enslavement conducted by imperialism."

It recommitted Soviet national power and energies to the achievement of world revolutionary goals: "The might of our state, its example and authority, and its activeness in the international arena are put at the service of the ideals of socialism, and gain ever greater importance for solving world problems in the interests of the toilers of all countries."

It should be emphasized that all of this ideological and rhetorical escalation was not accompanied by overt aggression in Soviet foreign policy. Nevertheless, it did signify a considerable disenchantment with Khrushchev's détente policy, which Brezhnev and others felt had played into the hands of the United States. The Soviet leaders, at this point, were intent on mobilizing Soviet public opinion and military power to redress the inequalities with Washington, to force a Vietnamese settlement favorable to Hanoi, and to deter the United States from possible intervention in other parts of the Third World.

The Troubled Waters of the Middle East

After Khrushchev's downfall, Soviet policy took an ominous turn in the Middle East, where some Soviet leaders saw an opportunity to make diplomatic gains at the expense of the United States. Soviet moves in the Middle East appeared to be coordinated with their encouragement of President Charles de Gaulle's animosity towards NATO.

Soviet diplomacy was rather active in both areas during 1967. In April, Premier Kosygin met with his Syrian counterpart in

Moscow and concluded an agreement to lend substantial help in construction of the Euphrates Dam. A half year later the U.S.S.R. and Syria were to sign an agreement for the development of Syrian oil resources. Kosygin and Admiral Gorshkov visited Cairo from May 10 to 18 for talks with U.A.R. President Gamal Nasser. Kosygin lauded the U.A.R., along with Algeria, Syria, and Iraq, as a model of revolutionary social development. Military discussions were cloaked in secrecy, but the subsequent increase in activity by the Soviet Mediterranean fleet makes it likely that an understanding was reached on naval facilities in Egypt.

There is considerable evidence to suggest that some Soviet leaders encouraged Nasser to adopt a more militant position towards Israel, ostensibly to deter Israel from attacking Syria in retaliation for acts of harassment and also perhaps for other reasons. Apparently Nasser was misled not only by faulty Soviet intelligence but also by assurances of Soviet assistance in the event of a war with Israel. At any rate, soon after Kosygin's departure from Cairo, Nasser announced that the Strait of Tiran would be closed to Israeli shipping and requested that U.N. patrols on Egyptian territory be withdrawn. A Soviet government statement of May 23 promptly rebuked Israel and "imperialist plotters" for belligerent acts in the region. The U.A.R. war minister and Syrian political leaders arrived in Moscow a few days later for consultation. Soviet warships entered the Mediterranean through the Dardanelles in greater strength than usual for the alleged purpose of "insuring the security of our southern borders" and counteracting the pressure on the Arab states exerted by the U.S. Sixth Fleet. There was informed speculation that Cairo and Damascus were incited by false intelligence reports from Moscow. This was heightened by the subsequent replacement of K.G.B. Chairman Semichastny by the Party Secretary Yu. V. Andropov.

As a result of these tensions generated by Syrian and Egyptian belligerence, Israel reacted in June by initiating a lightning war that simultaneously humiliated the Arab states and infuriated the Russians. Despite whatever assurances of support Moscow may have promised Nassar in May, the Soviet reaction did not go beyond symbolic military demonstrations and rhetorical flourishes in its propaganda and diplomacy. Moscow and the United States avoided possible confrontation out of prudence and mutual self-interest.

Although Soviet foreign policy suffered a defeat as the result of the six-day war, provoking fierce controversy within the Soviet Central Committee, the Brezhnev centrist position won out as the Central Committee adopted a resolution on June 20-21 approving the Politburo's handling of the Middle Eastern crisis. Diplomatic reports from Moscow suggested that Brezhnev was under fire in Soviet ruling circles for adventurism in foreign policy, but his grip on the party was strengthened by personnel changes made at and just after the June Plenum. The K.G.B. head Andropov, a regular travelling companion of Brezhnev, was admitted to the Politburo as a candidate member. Shelepin, a natural rival of Brezhnev in the Central Committee Secretariat, was demoted to full-time work in the trade union apparatus. V. V. Grishin, a candidate member of the Politburo whose record suggested adherence to Brezhnev, was transferred from the Trade Union Council to the first secretaryship of the Moscow City Party Committee. He displaced Yegorychev, a conservative critic of Brezhnev, generally thought to be part of the Shelepin "Komsomol Clique" within the Soviet leadership.

Since French reaction to the Israeli offensive paralleled that of Moscow, the Soviet leaders stepped up their policy of courting de Gaulle, thus furthering the split between Paris and Washington. Kosygin journeyed to the French capital in December 1967, returning de Gaulle's earlier state visit to Moscow. The Soviet premier welcomed de Gaulle's intention to sever ties with NATO and encouraged the French President to hope for closer economic and technical ties between France and the Eastern bloc. Kosygin's visit to Turkey later that month was also designed to draw Turkey away from the NATO Alliance.

After the June war, the Soviet Union engaged in much diplomatic activity in support of the Arab states. Moscow unswervingly supported the Arab position in the U.N., broke diplomatic relations with Israel, convoked a meeting of its Eastern

European allies and prevailed upon Bulgaria, Czechoslovakia, Hungary, Poland, and Yugoslavia to follow suit. (East Germany has no such ties with Israel. Rumania, which recently signed a four-year trade-and-payments agreement with Israel, held back.) Soviet President Podgorny and Army Chief of Staff Zakharov flew to Cairo on June 21 and assured Nasser of further diplomatic and military assistance. Soviet and allied leaders conferred on June 9 in Moscow and July 11-12 in Budapest, coordinating plans to rally world public opinion against continued Israeli occupation of Arab borderlands. The Rumanians attended the first meeting, but did not sign the fiercely partisan communique. They absented themselves from the Budapest meeting. (Ceausescu remarked in a speech to the Grand National Assembly on July 24 that Rumania's "differences of views" with other bloc countries "should in no way prevent friendly relations.") Kosygin argued the case of the Arab states at a special session of the U.N. General Assembly and during his nine-hour talk with President Johnson at Glassboro, N.J.

As a further gesture of Soviet support, Soviet naval units made an official visit to Alexandria on August 6-11. Inside the U.S.S.R. and Poland, in particular, an anti-Zionist propaganda campaign brought renewed intimidation of Jewish citizens. Charles Jordan, the American vice-president of a Jewish relief agency, was murdered while visiting Prague in August, and Czechoslovak secret police were generally thought to be responsible.

On March 29, 1968, Brezhnev, in his speech to the Moscow City Party Conference, indicated obliquely that Soviet foreign policy was in disarray. He said further economic sacrifices would be necessary, particularly now that Egypt's huge losses of military equipment had to be replaced. He appealed for "iron party discipline" and stressed the exclusive leading role of the party apparatus. He spoke of economic progress and military power in the same breath, warning those eager for a more rapid improvement of living standards that "it would be wrong to reduce everything to material incentives; this would impoverish the inner world of Soviet man." Reviewing world events, Brezhnev saw the possibility of a great economic crisis in the United States and

Western Europe. He condemned imperialism for trying to subvert communist governments by agitating "nationalistic" and "revisionist" elements. The Soviet party chief threatened severe punishment of "two-faced people" and "renegades" who flirted with noncommunist political ideas.

A regular plenary session of the C.P.S.U. Central Committee, supposedly called to deal with agriculture, was devoted instead to foreign bloc political and ideological affairs when it opened on April 9. On the basis of Brezhnev's report behind closed doors, a decree was adopted approving plans for a world communist conference in Moscow during November and December 1968. The decree went on to say that Moscow's German policy would remain one of "exposing revanchism and militarism" in the Federal Republic. The communist parties of Eastern Europe were expected to join the C.P.S.U. in struggle against West German imperialism. Internal censorship would be tightened because of ideological subversion by the western powers. Singled out as the biggest task of party and nation was the "further strengthening of the homeland's political, economic and defense power." This decree may be regarded as the most forceful assertion of the post-Khrushchev leadership's will to combat the erosion of its Marxist-Leninist system of belief and absolutist form of single-party rule.

The May Day slogans published in the Soviet press on April 17, 1968, afforded additional insight into the Kremlin's directives on global policy. Several slogans issued in April and October 1967 were changed and given an anti-western turn. "Struggle against imperialism" was added to the previous April's first slogan, and the significance of May Day was now the unity of "all anti-imperialist forces," not just "the working class." The priority of foreign over domestic tasks was indicated by omission of the previous October's notice, "The building of communism is our patriotic and international duty!" A more internationalist flavor was given to the slogan addressed to Soviet military personnel. They had earlier been asked to "stand guard over the achievements of the Great October Socialist Revolution and the achievements of socialism." Now the call was broadened to "be always ready to crush any aggressor." A slogan denouncing

West Germany, which had been dropped in October 1967, was resurrected.

It became more and more evident, however, that the Middle East failure had provoked ambivalent currents within the Soviet leadership. Soviet policy statements fluctuated between belligerence and moderation. Thus, on June 27, 1968, world attention was captured by Gromyko's remark to the Supreme Soviet that the Kremlin "is ready to enter an exchange of opinions" on "the mutual limitation and later reduction of strategic weapons, both offensive and defensive, including antimissiles." This statement came only a few days after the U.S. Senate authorized the construction of a "thin" SENTINEL antiballistic missile system. This ambivalence was further revealed by Brezhnev's guarded statement, in July 1968, that the U.S.-U.S.S.R. agreement to sign a nuclear non-proliferation treaty was "a document of peace that is aimed at reducing the danger of war."

On November 6, the keynote report of the Soviet Politburo for the 51st anniversary of the Bolshevik Revolution was delivered by First Deputy Premier Mazurov. He spoke of a basic cleavage between communist and noncommunist interests on the international scene. Soviet vigilance could not be diminished in view of "the further polarization of class and political forces in the world arena." Mazurov restated in ideological terms the Kremlin's universalist pretentions and hope to expand the area of its controlling influence, "Lenin foresaw that historical development will raise the problem of transforming the dictatorship of the proletariat from a national force into an international one, capable of exerting a decisive influence on the whole of world politics."

The changing balance of power in the Mediterranean was the subject of articles in *Izvestiva* and *Red Star* on November 11-12. Ideological and geopolitical reasons were offered for the Soviet's enlarged presence in the region. The global class struggle was said to have recently escalated and socialist forces were compelled to thwart capitalist intriguers bent on stifling the national liberation movements within the region. These developments had special significance for international communism because of the Sino-Soviet rivalry and border conflict.

IX.

The Sino-Soviet Controversy

The roots of today's Sino-Soviet controversy are buried in different cultures, histories, and a heightened mood of nationalism in both countries reinforced by memories of long-standing enmity. The cooperation that existed in the early post-World War II years was not enough to overcome friction produced by these forces.

The great divide is 1956 and Khrushchev's 20th Party Congress destalinization speech. The Chinese resented Khrushchev's denunciation of Stalin's position on peaceful coexistence and peaceful transition to socialism, as the general line of the international communist movement. They objected as well to his failure to consult Mao. The friction was compounded when Peking interjected itself into European bloc politics during the 1956 Eastern European revolutions. Allegedly Khrushchev urged intervention against Poland and the Chinese opposed it; then, when Khrushchev resisted intervention in Hungary, Peking favored it. Peking also objected to Moscow's courting India and extending its political activity into Asia.

While Moscow was beginning to shift its international policies, the Chinese left wing won the adoption of a radical domestic economic strategy. This was the Great Leap Forward and the People's Communes. Both nations were responding to their own independent needs. The Russians needed to modernize their economy and secure greater popular support. The Chinese needed to satisfy the vast opposition that surfaced in the short-lived "hundred flowers" campaign of 1957 and to move rapidly toward an industrial economy. But each struck out in an opposite direction.

Their differences became even more apparent at the Moscow Conference of November 1957. Cooperation was publicly emphasized. But Mao, speaking at this Conference one month after the launching of Sputnik, declared his view of the "East Wind prevailing over the West." He expressed guarded but optimistic conclusions about a shift in the strategic superiority of the communist nations over the noncommunists. Yet his warning against the twin dangers of slighting the enemy ("opportunism") and failing to take full account of its power ("adventurism") did not win the Kremlin's endorsement. In addition, Mao criticized Yugoslav revisionism. He did so at a time when Khrushchev had defeated Molotov on the Yugoslav question and when Moscow was seeking an accord with Tito.

In 1958 Chinese action in the Formosa Straits became a source of great friction. The Chinese were testing the U.S., but to Moscow the risks were too high and it was the wrong issue. Berlin and Western Europe ranked higher in Moscow's priorities. Though Khrushchev did support China, Moscow's assurances were issued only after Peking offered to negotiate on September 6.

In August 1959 came China's incursions into India, followed by the disgrace of Chinese Defense Minister Marshal Peng The-huai in September. Khrushchev's visit to the United States in September, his view of favorable relations with the United States, and his argument with Mao over communes, all rubbed the wrong way.

It was in June 1959, Peking says, that the Russians tore up the October 1957 agreement on technology for national defense and refused to provide China with a sample atomic bomb and technical data on its manufacture. Between 1957 and 1959 China began to see herself as having to go it alone. She also began to see Moscow as a power that would sacrifice Peking for its own objectives. A shake-up in Chinese military forces and strategies occurred. Peking began to place greater emphasis on insurrectionary activity. Peking shifted its attention to India and the south.

In 1959 the Chinese began to fish in the troubled waters of the world communist parties. Peking lobbied for support in the World Federation of Trade Unions at the Peking meeting in early June 1960 and at other international communist front meetings.

Peking's appeal to the sympathies of the Eastern European parties alarmed Moscow. Bitter recriminations were exchanged at the Rumanian Communist Party Conference in Bucharest in June 1960. Khrushchev labeled Mao another Stalin. Victory fell to neither Moscow nor Peking at the 81-party meeting in Moscow in November 1960, and the factional disputes continued. Moscow pressed for discipline and recognition of its leading role; Peking pressed for equality and a joint Sino-Soviet directorate for the whole movement.

Earlier in August 1960, when the Great Leap was manifesting its failure, Moscow withdrew Soviet technicians from China.

Though the Albanians and the Chinese became publicly aligned at the conference of 81 communist parties the following November, a facade of unity was maintained for almost a year. At the 22nd Congress of the Communist Party of the Soviet Union in October 1961, the charade was dropped. Chinese Prime Minister Chou En-lai openly rebuked Khrushchev for his criticism of Albania and laid a wreath on Stalin's remains, which were to be removed from Lenin's mausoleum a few days later.

In the summer of 1962, the Chinese and Russians clashed over: 1) Yugoslavia and revisionism, and 2) the Cuban missiles crisis. The Cuban dispute started over tactics, but mushroomed into bitter exchanges about their own border arrangements. In reply to the Chinese charge that Moscow was guilty of "adventurism" and "capitulationism" in the face of "imperialist nuclear blackmail," Khrushchev, reporting to the Supreme Soviet in December, sardonically noted that if imperialism was a "paper tiger," it was equipped with nuclear teeth. He baited Peking with parallels about China's withdrawal from Indian territory, and Peking's failure to liberate Hong Kong and Macao. Peking replied sharply. If China's humiliation was to be raised, Russia was numbered among the imperialist powers that had forced "unequal treaties" upon China. Peking ended with the warning that China had not presented its case yet.

After continuing debates in 1962 at various party congresses, polemics were temporarily halted. Bilateral talks were proposed by the Russians and entered into on February 21, 1963.

At this point the issue of racism was first raised. Just before the talks opened in Moscow in July, the Chinese provocatively aired all their old charges. The Russians replied and added that the Chinese had tried to prevent Russian and European participation at the 1963 Tanganyikan Afro-Asian Solidarity Conference on the grounds that "the whites have nothing to do here." Moscow also rebuked Peking for nonchalance about nuclear war, which China allegedly favored on the grounds that the destruction of the imperialist powers would follow, but that some Chinese would survive. Moscow retorted that this notion contained the primitive and false idea that communism meant only that a few people ate out of a common bowl.

The bilateral talks ended on July 20 without any agreement. On August 5 the treaty banning nuclear tests in the atmosphere was signed in Moscow. Peking denounced the treaty as a "dirty fraud," charging the Russians with double dealing. An aroused appeal of concern from the Italian and other communist parties over the bitterness of the debate had little effect. The Chinese soon turned down Khrushchev's offer to resume economic and technical cooperation, charging that Moscow used its economic strength to "bully" and dominate its allies.

Reports started coming in about serious incidents along the Chinese-Soviet border in Sinkiang Province. Kazakhs, Kirghiz, and other national groups live on both sides of that border. Both sides stated that since 1960 some tens of thousands of people had crossed into the Soviet Union. According to the Chinese, they were incited and coerced by Soviet agents; according to the Russians, they sought refuge from Chinese maltreatment. The Russians also accused Peking of numerous frontier violations.

In the polemics that raged, the border question became ever more important. In an interview reported in the Japanese press, Mao Tse-tung suggested that the Soviet Union should return the Kurile Islands to Japan; he sensed Soviet vulnerability on the whole question of Soviet frontiers. He talked of Soviet appropriation of part of Rumania, Poland, East Germany, Finland, and Mongolia. He noted that "a hundred years ago the region east of Baikal became Russian territory and, since then, Vladivostok,

Khabarovsk, Kamchatka and other places have become territory of the Soviet Union." China, he added, had not yet presented its reckoning for this.

Khrushchev responded on September 15. He warned that the frontiers of the Soviet Union were sacred. He bitingly asked what the Chinese were doing in Sinkiang, an area populated by a people ethnically different from the Chinese?

With the fall of Khrushchev, Brezhnev and Kosygin tried to patch up the rift with the Chinese but the differences were too great. No agreement was reached.

On October 16, in Sinkiang, China exploded her first atomic bomb and Chou En-lai appealed for a summit of all countries to disavow the nuclear weapons.

In 1965 the conflict with Moscow reached a new intensity. Anti-Soviet demonstrations in Peking began in March following the alleged suppression in Moscow of a Vietnam rally by Chinese students. Demonstrations continued throughout 1966 and 1967 until almost all students were either expelled or withdrawn. Also in 1965, 47 Chinese scientists working at the Joint Nuclear Research Institute at Dunba returned to Peking.

Both sides, in 1965, held the other responsible for the Indonesian Communist Party (P.K.I.) fiasco. Kosygin did visit Peking in February, and Mao did send anniversary greetings to Moscow in celebration of the Russian Revolution, but the dispute passed over into the field of international organizations when the Chinese called on the World Federation of Trade Unions at its October Congress in Warsaw to oppose "peaceful co-existence."

As the Cultural Revolution mushroomed in 1966, Peking again meddled in the politics of Eastern Europe, where a resurgence of nationalism was occurring and where a number of party leaders were maneuvering for greater autonomy. Polemics were exchanged at conferences in Czechoslovakia and Sofia. In June, Chou En-lai visited Albania and Rumania. He praised the Rumanians and encouraged them in their struggle against outside interference. On March 23, China refused a Soviet invitation to attend the 23rd Congress of the Communist Party of the Soviet

Union. In March they clashed over Vietnam and borders. A "secret" Soviet letter was leaked to fraternal parties that charged Peking with rejecting joint action in Vietnam, with hindering the transport of Soviet war materials, and with promoting frontier clashes. In December Foreign Minister Chen Yi informed a Brazilian journalist that Moscow had moved troops from Eastern Europe and had built up 13 divisions on the Chinese frontier.

In early 1967, Chinese demonstrations outside the Soviet embassy in Peking were of unprecedented size and duration. Soviet families were manhandled at the Peking airport on their way home. Sharp protests were exchanged, with Peking identifying the Kremlin leaders with Hitler, the Czar and Chiang Kai-shek.

China announced the explosion of her first hydrogen bomb on June 17.

In 1968, the final defeat of Lui Shao Chi and the Soviet invasion of Czechoslovakia were the focal points of sharp polemics.

Moscow and Peking, by early 1969, were suffering the most deterioration in relations since Mao came to power. From March onward, they charged each other with border violations along the Ussuri River and in other areas. These incidents were used to stir up new waves of anti-Soviet and anti-Chinese feelings, and to prepare each nation for mass military buildups and war scares. On June 18, talks started between the delegation of the Sino-Soviet Frontier Navigation Commission (set up in 1951) and agreement was reached on navigation of frontier rivers. But Sino-Soviet relations deteriorated further in the aftermath of the Conference on World Communist Parties in Moscow in June. China was not formally condemned, but in the course of the debates the "Mao clique" was roundly denounced. Nevertheless, Kosygin visited Peking following the funeral of Ho Chi Minh in Hanoi, and large-scale talks were begun in October.

The border problem has a deep historical past with long precommunist roots. The Chinese grievances date from the Treaty of Nerchinsk (1689). It established the Sino-Soviet frontier along the Stanovoi Mountains, which form the watershed between the Amur and the Lena Rivers. In 1858 the Russians succeeded in having the weakened Manchu dynasty sign the Treaty of Aigun, ceding to Russia all the territory (about 185,000 square miles) on the left bank of the Amur. Thus, settlements at Hailanpao, Khabarovsk, and Nikolayevak were recognized by China as Russian. In 1860 both powers signed the Treaty of Peking. Under it, Russian occupation of the land eastward of the Ussuri to the coast was confirmed. Russia thus gained an enormous piece of land, which included, at its southern tip, the site of Vladivostok.

The Chinese, according to Hong Kong reports, do not expect the return of the land. They are, however, seeking Soviet acknowledgement of the Russian imposition of these "unequal treaties."

The Russians, in turn, refuse to yield. They are associating the present "eastern threat" with the nomadic incursions of the Mongols in the 13th century. They further reply that Chinese territorial demands are pure chauvanism and the Chinese have repeatedly violated the Sino-Soviet boundaries. They continuously warn that the frontiers of the Soviet Union are sacred and that anyone who dares to violate them will meet with a "resolute rebuff." The war scare of September 1969 has been eased; Moscow and Peking started high-level negotiations in October, but the talks have not modified the posture of either nation.

The military buildups continue. Thirty or more Soviet divisions, moved to the Chinese frontier in the summer of 1969, still stand poised in strike positions. Hardly more than two years ago the Soviets had 12 or 13 divisions deployed along their frontier with China. Of these, it is estimated, only two were full strength divisions. At that time, moreover, there were no Soviet units of any consequence in Outer Mongolia. Today the frontier divisions have been brought up to full strength, are deployed in Outer Mongolia, and are armed with artillery, rockets, aircraft, and all the equipment necessary for waging a conventional or nuclear war. The change in military buildup is striking.

In China, underground air-raid shelters are being built, grain stockpiled, troops moved to border regions, and people, even the youngest school children, are being drilled in protective measures again nuclear war. So intense is the hostility that the Chinese charge they are confronted not with a friendly communist ally, but with a hereditary enemy. They warn their people that Russia has embarked on a policy to destroy China, not only as a communist power but as a nation.

Thus, Moscow and Peking stand today much as they did in the 19th century, as traditional enemies. But the situation is more complex. They are arguing not only over national frontiers but ideologies and conflicting interests as well. With a quarrel that is a mix of nationalism, asymmetrical interests, and ideology, only a change in international politics and hard negotiations by cooperative Chinese and Russian diplomats can bring about the return of that brief and temporary period of friendship that they enjoyed immediately after World War II.

X.

The Triangulation of Global Power

Any realistic assessment of the prospects for international stability
will depend to an increasingly large extent upon the growing power
of China and the intensity and scope of her ambitions as a world
power.

For the moment, Chinese aspirations and behavior pose a
greater threat to the Soviet position than to the American, and
Peking may ultimately aim to attain a position from which she
can cripple the Soviet ambition to be an effective global com-
petitor with the United States, just as she has successfully crippled
the Soviet leadership of the world communist movement. Soviet-
American relations are thus an integral part of a complex triangular relationship among Moscow, Peking and Washington, in
which cause and effect have become inextricably merged and in-
capable of being disentangled. The behavior and conduct of each
state has a multiplier impact upon the reactions and responses of
the other partners in the triangle.

This strange triangular relationship was apparently set into
motion as far back as the days of the "Spirit of Geneva" in 1955.
Although the United States was unaware of its intimate involvement as a third party in a fragile Sino-Soviet partnership until
after the Cuban missile crisis in 1962, it then became clear that
U.S. behavior and intentions could be viewed as the single greatest
factors affecting Sino-Soviet relations. Unwittingly, U.S. responses
and reactions were registering on Sino-Soviet relations and the
center of a world revolutionary movement. Soviet leaders were
finally confronted with the moment of elementary contradictory
truth. Pursuing world revolution could only maximize the prospects of total physical annihilation as both a state and the center

of a messianic movement, and Moscow had to choose between survival and doctrinal virtue.

Ironically enough, continued Sino-Soviet hostility is likely to encourage Soviet tractability elsewhere. Because of its geographical position, the Soviet Union is peculiarly vulnerable to an encirclement strategy. As long as China sustains its hostility, Moscow cannot afford to antagonize its western neighbors, for fear of some nightmarish Sino-German coordination of pressure, if not actual collaboration, against the Soviet Union. The inopportune Chinese military incursion in the Soviet Far East in 1969, just as Moscow was reapplying pressure on West Berlin, may have been an esoteric Chinese bid to Bonn for informal cooperation. Moscow, a capital not unversed in the nuances and subtleties of esoteric communication, lost no time in sounding out Bonn about the state of Sino-German relations, noting in particular that West Germany is China's most active trading partner in the west. The quick relaxation of Soviet pressure on Berlin, however, was certainly not unnoticed by Bonn, whose leaders soothingly assured Ambassador Tsarapkin that West Germany would not seek to exploit Soviet difficulties with the Chinese, which, of course, could be interpreted as a threat as well as a promise.

The Chinese danger thus serves to encourage Soviet leaders to seek some sort of accommodation with the United States. At the same time, the Soviets probably realize that their open paranoia concerning China exposes them to some serious vulnerabilities. For example, the United States may find a vested interest in sustaining and aggravating Sino-Soviet relations in order to dampen Soviet appetites for adventures elsewhere.

As long as China is hostile to the Soviet Union, Moscow retains a vested stake in the perpetuation of Sino-American hostility. A rapprochement between Peking and Washington would enable the Chinese to concentrate their full fury against the Russians. A Chinese-American reconciliation is by no means considered an impossibility by Moscow. Significantly, the Soviet press has charged on more than one occasion that the Chinese leaders are plotting a rapprochement with the United States, and Soviet writers condemn with unusual vigor any intimation by western writers or spokesmen that a Sino-American rapprochement might be a distinct possibility. On the other hand, Taipei has expressed concern that the turmoil on the Chinese mainland might precipitate a joint Soviet-American intervention resulting in what is characterized as another Yalta, a Russo-American deal at China's expense. And in March 1969, Peking made the strange charge that the visit of Soviet journalist Victor Louis to Taiwan was part of a scheme to collude with Chiang Kai-shek against Peking. The Soviet fear of a Sino-German and a Sino-American rapprochement directed against Moscow has become a recurrent theme in the Soviet press since March 1969. Since a Sino-American rapprochement will be determined by Washington and Peking and not by Moscow, one of the genuine fears of some Soviet leaders is that such a rapprochement might enable China to devote greater attention to its unredeemed territories in the north.

The peculiar fluidity of Sino-Soviet-American relations has seriously complicated the impact of the Vietnamese war on future international stability. Khrushchev had virtually abandoned Vietnam; his successors reasserted Moscow's presence for complex reasons, some of them contradictory. Such presence would give Moscow a measure of control over the situation and an opportunity to claim credit in the event of its successful resolution. It was probably part of a plan designed to reduce or eliminate the sources of Sino-Soviet friction. But since Khrushchev's successors were just as adamant in pursuing the détente, although in a different form, the Soviet olive branch to China was rebuffed. The war in Vietnam escalated and Moscow became the chief supplier of arms to her North Vietnamese ally.

The Soviet leaders have exerted their influence both in favor of negotiated settlement of the war and in favor of its continuance on terms that weakened the United States. For some time the proponents of expanded Soviet-American détente viewed the war as an obstacle to improved relations. As the war intensified and was prolonged, and as suspicion of the Johnson Administration's intent increased, however, sentiment in the Politburo shifted. Relations with both Peking and Washington seemed to have deteriorated and the Soviet perspective on Vietnam became ambiguous. To some Soviet leaders, the war remained an insuperable barrier to expanded cooperation. To others, the inconclusive character of an intensified conflict, which strained U.S. economic and military resources, aroused domestic agitation, and diverted U.S. attention away from other areas. This appeared to pay greater dividends than would a settlement. Also, the war close to China's borders kept Peking off balance. Thus, Moscow exploited the war by exacting informal and implicit concessions from the United States concerning Eastern Europe, while making some efforts toward ending the war.

Since the advent of the Paris talks, the Vietnamese war has become essentially a peripheral factor in Soviet-American relations, although the Nixon Administration is still relying on Moscow to influence Hanoi towards an acceptable conclusion of the conflict.

XI.

The Temptations and Risks of Strategic Superiority

The Soviet Union is irrevocably committed to function on the world stage as a global power. But the precise contours of that role have by no means been delineated. In the near future, it is likely that the Soviet leaders will avoid pressing confrontations with the United States in peripheral areas and instead will use international organizations and conferences as their prime instruments of policy. It is noteworthy that the Soviet leaders, despite their extensive commitments, have permitted the Arab-Israeli conflict to be diverted into the United Nations rather than allow it to force them into direct confrontation with the United States. It is not likely, however, that either Soviet-American relations or Sino-Soviet relations can be usefully aired in international bodies.

The decisive factor in international stability, of course, remains the state of relations between the United States and the Soviet Union. This, in turn, depends in large measure upon the Soviet leadership's perceptions of Washington's intentions and capabilities as measured against their own purposes and power. The Soviet leadership appears sorely divided over the precise character that Soviet-American relations should assume. Some, including Kosygin apparently, seem to favor a continuation and expansion of the détente ushered in by the partial test-ban treaty of 1963. Others may wish to challenge the United States overtly for primacy in the international system. Still others, perhaps including Brezhnev, perceive a limited or arrested détente as the best formula to assure the sanctity of the status quo in Europe, which Moscow would like to preserve while freeing the Soviet Union to alter it elsewhere. A fourth possibility, *entente,* may appeal to sectors of the Soviet intelligentsia and to intellectuals like Andrei Sakharov; but it is not likely that the Soviet leaders can see it as a real possibility at the present time, and their debate probably revolves around the first three alternatives.

During the five years of the Johnson Administration, the Soviet leadership, on balance, probably felt that international stability worked to the advantage of the United States in particular and the status quo in general. Since international stability is inherently anti-revolutionary, a stable world is one in which the Soviet Union surrenders the political and diplomatic initiative to the United States as the paramount power and the chief guardian of the status quo. In the Johnson era, the Soviet position in world affairs was diminished to that of a tired, worn-out revolutionary power content with permanent secondary status, while the United States was left free to flex its diplomatic and military muscles all over the world. While the Johnson Administration faithfully refrained from overt hostile moves against the Soviet position in Eastern Europe, its selective enticement of individual communist states left the unimaginative Soviet leaders defenseless, except for resort to military intervention to arrest the growing forces of autonomy. Furthermore, during the Johnson years, the Soviet Union saw China progressively transformed from an alienated ally into a hostile and threatening neighbor, the world communist movement fractured and demoralized, and the national liberation movement deprived of its protective umbrella.

Confident of its superior power and relying on the Soviet Union to refrain from any action that might endanger Soviet-American collaboration, the United States massively escalated the war in Vietnam, systematically bombed Moscow's ally, and landed Marines in the Dominican Republic to prevent the establishment of a revolution-oriented regime. Furthermore, not only in Moscow, but also in Belgrade, Cairo and elsewhere (particularly after the Arab-Israeli War of 1967) the impression achieved widespread acceptance that the Johnson Administration had been using détente, not to preserve international stability, but to disguise a political offensive against Soviet and radical nationalist positions throughout the world. The Dominican affair, the ouster of Sukarno in Indonesia and of Goulart in Brazil, the fall of Nkrumah, the overthrow of Ben Bella in Algeria, the Greek military take-over and finally the Israeli attack upon Egypt appeared to many in Moscow as part of an overall U.S. design. Nasser openly complained in Cairo that the chief danger to peace and progress was the absence of any force that could deter or contain the United States. The Italian communist paper, *Rinascita*, flatly claimed that the Johnson Administration was pursuing a cleverly concealed "roll back" policy:

> For the policy of the status quo and the attempts to divide the world into zones of influence between the two super-powers, U.S. imperialism is gradually substituting a revised and corrected re-edition of the old policy of *roll back*, giving birth, within the framework of nuclear co-existence with the U.S.S.R. (caused by reasons of *force majeure*), to a series of local interventions (economic, political, military) designed to modify the world equilibrium by means of setting up reactionary regimes, or by support given to them, and liquidation of the progressive forces and movements in individual countries.

One of the constants of the world situation during the post-war period, up to the past year or two, had been the clearcut U.S. superiority in thermonuclear capability. It had apparently fostered stability, but a stability which the Soviet leaders may have perceived favoring U.S. interests. This raised in the Soviet mind the entire question of whether the United States was deceptively palming off a condition of disequilibrium in its favor as international stability.

The Brezhnev-Kosygin regime, soon after taking office, embarked upon an accelerated program of narrowing or eliminating the U.S. lead in strategic nuclear striking power, not only by stepping up the production of ICBMs, improving and refining existing weapons, hardening launching sites, and expanding naval capability, but also by deploying a modest ABM system around Moscow. It is obvious, therefore, that the present Soviet leaders are convinced that the elimination of the strategic gap is a necessary prerequisite to an effective policy of deterring the United States from playing world policeman. On the other hand, the dominant view of the U.S. administration from about 1963 until 1969 was that the United States possessed an invulnerable deterrent force, an "assured destruction capability" vis-à-vis the U.S.S.R., which would not be eroded by the Soviet achievement of strategic nuclear parity. While this view was not without its detractors, there had been an equally forceful view that the achievement of parity would contribute to a more stable mutual deterrence, improving the chances for arms control and other agreements. Parity, it was argued, would eliminate the essentially psychological and symbolic sense of inferiority in Moscow without simultaneously affecting the actual power equilibrium. The reappraisal of the strategic nuclear balance in the Nixon administration has raised other views, including the fear that the loss of strategic advantage by the United States might in time have a sharply contrary result. Soviet leaders could believe that the time had come to settle outstanding political issues in favor of the Soviet Union, and the Soviet military might be used to greater political advantage under the nuclear umbrella.

We really do not know to what extent the strategic superiority of the United States was the decisive factor enabling it to behave with relative impunity in peripheral areas of the world while simultaneously deterring vigorous Soviet action. This includes Soviet action not only against its own recalcitrant client states in Eastern Europe but also in other areas, i.e., deterring a possible Soviet intervention in the Arab-Israeli war to prevent the ignominious defeat of its Arab client states. We also do not know to what extent the Soviet moves against Czechoslovakia and the threatening gestures against Rumania and Yugoslavia were the reflection of a greater confidence inspired by the relative growth of its missile and nuclear power. As the Soviet Union's strategic military power grew, Moscow could manifest less self-restraint in its behavior.

The assumption that the Soviet leaders seek parity as an ultimate goal in order to establish symbolic equality with the United States—and as a necessary prerequisite to negotiations as equals on other issues—bears careful scrutiny. Some Soviet leaders may have subscribed to this view, but others probably have not. The crucial unknown is the degree to which a significant element in the Soviet leadership believes that Soviet strategic superiority is a feasible goal, and that its achievement will transfer the initiative to Moscow and bring about a reversal of roles between the two global powers. It is an unpalatable but ineluctable fact that the Soviet Union is now in a better position to strive for superiority.

Given the resources and capabilities of the United States, the Soviet proponents of parity may well warn the advocates of superiority that the Soviet Union cannot hope to win an accelerated arms race without straining its economy, provoking internal discontent as a consequence, and forever forfeiting an opportunity to reach substantial agreements on the basis of equality. But the advocates of superiority might well make the following argument: The United States is now psychologically, militarily and politically on the defensive. The general mood in the United States is strongly in favor of détente and disentanglement. Bruised and humiliated by the Vietnamese war, alienated from its allies in Western Europe as a consequence, and wracked by internal racial disorders, youthful rebellions, conflict between rich and poor, and afflicted by political malaise and war weariness, America, regardless of its administration, cannot confidently hope to mobilize the necessary social support and political unity to engage in a more vigorous arms race, without aggravating these internal contradictions. Furthermore, the argument might run, the U.S. position in the Third World has been discredited by its counter-revolutionary interventionism. A strategically superior Soviet Union could not but revive the morale of revolutionary forces, regimes, and movements in under-developed countries, frighten America's NATO allies into opting for neutrality, isolate West Germany, solidify the Soviet position in Eastern Europe, reunify the world communist movement, force Israel into a dictated settlement with the Arab states, and place China on notice that Moscow is not to be trifled with. While such a policy could run the risk of encouraging a mutually defensive Sino-American rapprochement, the view might hold that it is even more likely that China, confronted with a powerful Russia, would alter its attitude towards the Soviet Union, particularly if Mao Tse-tung passes from the scene in the meantime.

Will the Soviet choose such a policy? If it does seem a real alternative, considerable responsibility must be placed upon the Johnson Administration for demonstrating that strategic superiority does indeed make a difference. In spite of the fact that the Soviet Union possessed an "invulnerable" second strike with "assured" destructive capabilities, the capability of a strategically inferior Russia was of a limited character as compared with the nearly *absolute* level of "assured" destructive capability possessed by the United States, and it was this imbalance that made the difference.

The diplomatic utility of strategic superiority, defined as a unilateral first strike capability, should not be obscured by the miasma of controversy generated over the rationality or irrationality of nuclear war. As an instrument of diplomatic blackmail, strategic superiority apparently retains its effectiveness. Such a capability can be a powerful factor in the deterrence and paralysis of responses to military and diplomatic initiatives in areas marginal to the interests of the global powers. The Soviet leaders may opt for a first strike capability, not necessarily for the purpose of launching and winning a nuclear war with the United States, but in order to escalate the risks of American counter-action to Soviet initiatives. Strategic superiority thus could provide a kind of protective umbrella for Soviet diplomatic maneuvers and would enable Moscow to maximize her options in foreign policy.

If it is a prime current objective of the Soviet Union to contain and deter U.S. power rather than to erode or roll it back, then the achievement of strategic parity might be sufficient to pursue this goal. It appears that the Nixon Administration is seriously contemplating a reduction in U.S. international obligations. Agreements on arms control designed to stabilize the existing distribution of power might well offer a welcome respite to both parties. Unfortunately, however, parity as a concept and as a reality is not subject to the precise, calibrated measurement required to make it a mutually acceptable formula. Superiority, in contrast, is much easier to measure and define, particularly when the margin is substantial. The inability to arrive at a mutually satisfactory definition of parity may constitute an insuperable roadblock to agreement, even though both parties might be willing to accept it in principle. As a consequence, the temptation for either Washington or Moscow or both to strive for a measurable degree of superiority may be unavoidable.

Even if the Soviets choose parity, and assuming that an acceptable formula is devised for strategic arms control, it is not likely that the Soviet Union will abandon its role as a global power. Although Moscow might conceivably accept a freeze on missile or atomic weapons and even accept partial cutbacks in strategic force levels, the Soviet leaders will continue to develop conventional military capabilities sufficient to enable them to compete with the United States on a global scale. This means that the Soviet leaders will need an expanded naval force—helicopter and possibly aircraft carriers, naval infantry (marines)—and long-range air troop carriers to enable them to provide sufficient forces either to deter the United States from intervening or to permit their own intervention. This also suggests that the Soviet Union will continue to seek to acquire the use of foreign ports and bases in friendly countries in the Mediterranean, the Indian Ocean and Southeast Asia. Latin America, except for Cuba, will probably remain off-limits for the time being, but this does not exclude a little Soviet "bridge-building" in reverse, and "peaceful engagement" with Latin American regimes of various political tendencies. The current flirtation with Peru may become a good example of future Soviet behavior. While such an evolutionary policy might infuriate Castro and Latin American revolutionaries, it will nevertheless serve the interests of Moscow as a global power by weakening the U.S. position in Latin America.

The area of possible Soviet-American agreement remains fairly large, but perhaps it has contracted somewhat from earlier possibilities. In any event, it is under constant scrutiny by more skeptical members of the Politburo. Even during the grimmest period of U.S. escalation in Vietnam, the Soviet leadership entered into a number of agreements with the United States, the most important of which was the nonproliferation treaty. Various bilateral agreements were signed in the immediate past. These include cultural exchange programs, treaties on outer space, the consular agreement, the Moscow-New York air agreement, and the important agreement adopted as a resolution of the Security Council on June 19, 1968, whereby the United States and the Soviets jointly agree to assist nonnuclear powers threatened or attacked with nuclear weapons.

Both the United States and Russia will probably reaffirm the sanctity of their respective spheres of influence, the latest manifestation of this tacit agreement being the mild American reaction to the Czech events. The questions of bridge-building and peaceful-engagement, however, remain moot for the moment.

In the Middle East, Russia and the United States appear to be moving in the direction of an imposed settlement, whose outlines remain obscure. Moscow will continue to expand its involvement in the Arab world, providing more credible and effective guarantees against another Israeli attack. What the Soviet leaders will do if the Arab states take the initiative or if a conflict breaks out accidentally, remains uncertain. Apparently this is one of the most controversial issues in the Politburo, with some members encouraging the Arabs and others counseling caution.

In the Far East, Moscow still appears to have more of an interest in ending the Vietnamese war than in seeing it continue, despite the obvious usefulness of having a large American military force on the Asian mainland to the south of China. Moscow's relative indifference to the destruction of the Indonesian Communist Party and its support to Pakistan and India are reaffirmations of its Chinese encirclement policy. Here, the key to Soviet success largely depends upon the United States, and Sino-American relations may turn out to be the most important determinant of Soviet behavior elsewhere.

Since the Soviet Union is too powerful to refrain from challenging the United States, we can expect continued rivalry between the global powers during the next decade, but it will assume increasingly traditional patterns. The evolution of European relations may act as a barometer of such change.

XII.

Eastern Europe Since Czechoslovakia

The Soviet-led invasion of Czechoslovakia in August 1968 not only shattered some illusions, but it also upset some widely held calculations about Moscow's predictability. These calculations, though articulated mainly by western analysts, were also probably shared by certain influential circles in Eastern Europe, including the ruling circles of some states. They probably were used to furnish a guide for predicting Soviet responses to courses of action they might be contemplating.

The most relevant of these calculations was based on the belief that Moscow, aware of the immense political risks involved, would refrain from armed intervention against even the most troublesome Eastern European ally, provided that ally abided by two cardinal rules: 1) continued membership in the Warsaw Pact alliance; 2) internal maintenance of the "socialist system," organizationally expressed through communist, one-party domination. The crucial corollary to this was the growing assumption that the prerogative of judging whether these two rules were being obeyed had been passing steadily from Moscow to the leadership of the state concerned. This assumption had grown only gradually and at times had been seriously shaken. But, by 1968, it must have seemed reasonably well established as a working principle in relations between the Soviet Union and its Eastern European allies.

This was the calculation on which Rumanian defiance of the Soviet Union was based; later it sustained the Dubcek leadership in Czechoslovakia in its pursuit of new policies both at home and abroad. It should be stressed that the assumption implied immunity only against armed intervention, not reprobation, threats, ostracism, attempted subversion, or a variety of economic sanctions. All these the Soviet Union and some of its loyalist allies had already used against Rumania; some were also used against the new Czechoslovak regime. But a liberalized or divergent regime, untied, confidently led, and enjoying popular support, could withstand such pressure. Rumania had shown this; even Czechoslovakia, though not so united or confidently led, would also have shown it. Safe from the ultimate sanction of armed force, such a regime could proceed on its own road to socialism and act on its own interpretation of membership in the Soviet-dominated alliance system.

The calculation proved wrong. All that can be said for it now is that it was never unreasonable. It took into account several factors: Khrushchev's pragmatism in coping with Eastern Europe's national diversity; the evolution, demonstrable in many ways, of the Soviet bloc toward a more traditional type of alliance with the usual stresses and strains; The Soviet Union's need to make credible to the people of noncommunist democracies its proposals for European security and arms agreements with the United States; The preoccupation of Khrushchev's successors with the accumulation of domestic problems and; The apparent necessity for Moscow to show a clean face to an increasingly restive and critical world communist movement.

The experience of the Soviet decision to invade Czechoslovakia, however, has shown most clearly that the interests, feelings, and considerations of foreign communist parties, at least those of the Western European communist parties, are not taken into account. The communist parties in both Italy and France made it quite clear that they strongly disapproved of any unilateral and military solution of the Czechoslovakian problem. Moreover, they had a very positive stake in the success of the Czechoslovakian experiment, which gave them hope of being attractive to new groups of voters and of being included in national coalition governments, i.e., a new communist model might give them the chance to come to power which they had been longing for since 1947. The Soviet leadership not only disregarded their wishes in handling the Czechoslovakians, but it did almost anything to offend them.

What the disproved calculation failed to take into account was mainly the will and ability of the leadership of the Soviet Party apparatus to survive. The word "survive" is important. Having shown a strong unwillingness to adapt to the challenges and demands of the '60s, this apparatus was now bent mainly on survival. Its method was resistance rather than genuine reform—resistance to the disruptive trends discernible in Eastern Europe. These trends were already beginning to appear in the Soviet Union itself.

It was this apparatus backlash that unseated Khrushchev in 1964. Since then, the party-first policy has continued under his successors. The invasion of Czechoslovakia was only the most spectacular and illustrative example of that policy. Strategic and security considerations, the fear of West German ideological, if not military encroachment in Czechoslovakia, were, of course, important factors influencing the Soviet decision to invade. So was the Czechoslovakian concept of a community of interests among the countries of Central Europe. This concept was most embarrassing to Moscow. The possibility arose that the Federal Republic, until then a much-scolded devil, could gain general attractiveness as a partner of Eastern communist nations. Such an eventuality seemed hardly tolerable to the Soviet leaders, both with a view to West Germany's role in NATO and to the Soviet desire to keep its hegemony over Eastern Europe.

When the Soviet leadership decided to invade Czechoslovakia, it had to look forward to the rather certain possibility of NATO's being strengthened. The fact that a decision was taken nevertheless strongly indicates that the consolidation of a Soviet hegemony in Eastern Europe had taken precedence over the anti-NATO aims connected with European security policies.

But these considerations served only to reinforce the central factor, which was the fear of the Soviet apparatus. There was also division in the Soviet Politburo over the decision to invade, indicating that cooler heads still survive in the top leadership. But a majority concurred in the invasion. Its execution was an awesome demonstration of the resilence of the apparatus mentality. Until there is sufficient evidence that this mentality, and its representatives, have ceased to influence Soviet decision-making, then it would be dangerous to dismiss the Czechoslovak invasion as an isolated aberration that cannot be repeated.

XIII.

Soviet Policy Aims in Eastern Europe

The night of August 20-21, 1968, re-emphasized a truth that was perhaps lost sight of in the preceding years: Eastern Europe is of vital importance in Soviet foreign policy. In periods when the situation there is relatively calm, as between 1957 and 1968, and since the Czechoslovak invasion, Eastern Europe takes its place in the whole spectrum of Soviet foreign policy considerations. Only in what is judged a direct emergency—Czechoslovakia—does it take absolute precedence.

If the Soviet Union is really seeking a permanent grip on Eastern Europe, it will have to resort to heavy political pressure and, in the case of Rumania and Yugoslavia, perhaps to further military action. This could immeasurably increase the difficulties of achieving détente with the west and might even endanger an adequate degree of protection against China.

If NATO policy were firm enough, any arrangement with the Soviet Union on European security need not lead either to a tightened Soviet grip on Eastern Europe or to the minimization of the American presence in Western Europe. Moreover, an arrangement on arms stability, if it is to be truly lasting, cannot be separated from the basic undesirability of the status quo in Europe, which the Soviet Union is doing its best to legitimize. This is not just a moral linkage but a military one as well. The United States, for one, has strategic responsibilities in Europe depending, to a considerable degree, on how the Soviets see their own interests and position their own forces.

The contradiction between insuring Soviet authority in Eastern Europe and arriving at a European security arrangement within the framework of a general détente has profoundly affected

Soviet policy in Europe since 1963 or 1964. Détente has tended to work against discipline in the Eastern bloc and, conversely, discipline there has tended to work against détente. Moscow has been aware of this and, despite Czechoslovakia, has sought to avoid having to impose its will, since the invasion, through iron ruthlessness.

Eastern European economic reform, fueled by general economic retardation and periodic economic crises, poses other contradictions. Once steps toward flexible prices, optimal planning, and market-simulating management are taken, economic reform measures may prove relatively irreversible. Technological backwardness and ineffective planning and management seem to doom many of the Eastern European economies to disappointing performance unless serious changes are made.

Soviet policy, however, has exercised a restraining influence on Eastern European economic change. The central question is whether short and long run improvements in economic performance can be obtained without the necessity of changes having political effects beyond the limit of Soviet tolerance. Czech reforms preceding the Soviet military intervention in 1968 presumably exceeded tolerable limits by altering the role of the Czechoslovak Communist Party in Czech society and by pursuing an independent relationship with noncommunist nations, particularly economic relations with West Germany. That the changes in Hungarian planning and management seem to parallel the Czech reform, although with less visible and explicit political reform, suggests a measure of Soviet tolerance. The Rumanian foreign economic policy exceeded the Czech trading relations, but it may have had fewer joint financing and management aspects, and this, too, suggests the boundaries the Czechs may have exceeded.

China adds a new complexity and poses important questions for Soviet policy in Eastern Europe. If Moscow feels relations with China will become so tense as to demand a much greater degree of military, political, and psychological preparedness on its eastern flank, how will it seek to secure its western flank? By reducing its disciplinary ambitions in Eastern Europe and accepting a rapprochement between the two halves of Europe? Or by intensifying its discipline over its European allies, even at the cost of tension with the west?

Such contradictions as these may pose a dilemma for Soviet foreign policy makers. But it is just possible that Moscow could, for the near future, achieve its prime aim of tightened control over Eastern Europe. At the same time, it could go a long way toward achieving an advantageous détente with the west, including a virtual legitimization of the territorial status quo in Europe. In Soviet policy, however, such a détente would not preclude efforts to upset the political status quo in Western Europe on the assumption that the west, and particularly the United States, would not write off Eastern Europe, politically and morally. How valid is this assumption?

The Moscow leadership might well have been encouraged by American reaction to the invasion of Czechoslovakia and, more recently, by Washington's apparent lack of response to the deposition of Alexander Dubcek. Moscow might be moved to offer what the west would consider as concessions—such as American participation in an all-European security arrangement—in return for clear western recognition of Eastern Europe as a Soviet sphere of domination. Similarly, in Asia, the danger from China may not escalate for some time to the point where it would seriously impede Soviet aims and methods in Europe.

It would indeed be ironic if such a constellation of events and circumstances transpired. It would mean that the Soviet party apparatus, pursuing a course at home and in Eastern Europe that was obscurantist and reactionary, had not only legitimized that course but had also gained a brilliant diplomatic victory, appearing as an enlightened seeker after peace and stability.

XIV.

Soviet Control Tightened in Eastern Europe

Soviet efforts to tighten control in Eastern Europe since August 1968 have resulted in a number of specific proposals and also have been given ideological and programmatic justification to the so-called Brezhnev doctrine. First enunciated in a *Pravda* commentary in September 1968, paraphrased by Foreign Minister Gromyko in the UN debate on Czechoslovakia the next month, and propounded once again by *Pravda* in April 1969, this doctrine reasserted what had been implicit under Stalin: Moscow (in consultation with its communist allies) has the right to determine whether the foreign or domestic policies of any of its allies are truly socialist or not. It also implicitly claims the right to take necessary action when any of its allies is deemed not to be pursuing socialist policies. The most relevant part of the doctrine as expounded by Sergei Kovalev in *Pravda* in September 1968 prior to its subsequent reformulation by the General Secretary is as follows:

> There is no doubt that the peoples of the socialist countries and the communist parties have, and must have, freedom to determine their country's path of development. However, any decision of theirs must damage neither socialism in their own country nor the fundamental interest of the other socialist countries, nor the worldwide workers' movement, which is waging a struggle for socialism. This means that every Communist party is responsible not only to its own people, but also to all the socialist countries and to the entire communist movement. Whoever forgets this is placing sole emphasis on the autonomy and independence of communist parties, lapsing

into one-sidedness, and shirking his international obligation . . . (*Pravda,* September 26, 1968)

Brezhnev, speaking to the Polish Communist Party Congress in November 1968 cast the doctrine in the following terms:

. . . The C.P.S.U. has always advocated that each socialist country determine the specific forms of its development along the road to socialism with consideration for its specific national conditions. However, it is known, comrades, that there are also common laws governing socialist construction, a deviation from which might lead to a deviation from socialism as such. And when the external and internal forces hostile to socialism seek to reverse the development of any socialist country toward the restoration of the capitalist order, when a threat to the cause of socialism in that country, a threat to the security of the socialist community as a whole, emerges, this is no longer only a problem of the people of that country but also a common problem, a concern for all socialist states. It goes without saying that such an action as military aid to a fraternal country to cut short the threat to the socialist order is an extraordinary step. It can be sparked off only by direct actions of the enemies of socialism inside the country and beyond its boundaries, actions creating a threat to the common interests of the camp of socialism. . . . (p. 4)

It would be dangerous for the Eastern European states, and unwise for the west, to assume that this was an ad hoc justification of the Czechoslovakia venture rather than a statement of general policy. Until the Brezhnev doctrine is repudiated, superseded or clearly allowed to lapse, it will provide the theoretical basis for Soviet domination of Eastern Europe. It might be too alarmist to consider it a hard and fast guide to Soviet action in the future, a law requiring armed intervention on all occasions when any Eastern European regime strays from Moscow's narrow path. But it can always be used as a weapon of intimidation and, in the last analysis, as a doctrine to legitimize another punitive invasion.

Soviet policy in Eastern Europe since August 1968 has evidently aimed at using intimidation, by the example of the Czech invasion and by the precept of the Brezhnev Doctrine, to consolidate Moscow's control. Soviet policy has sought three main objectives:

First, it is seeking to rejuvenate and restructure the Warsaw Pact, presumably through the establishment of some form of supranational authority over its members. Since August there has been an unusual amount of activity and consultation within the Pact, both at the military and political levels. In September, the Pact's military commander-in-chief, Marshall Ivan Yakubovski, visited the capitals of all the member countries; a meeting of the Pact defense ministers took place in October and the annual meeting of Pact representatives followed in Bucharest between November 26 and 28, 1968. Subsequently, intense, behind-the-scenes consultations are believed to have taken place in which Soviet proposals for strengthening the Pact were discussed. This culminated in the Warsaw Pact summit meeting in March 1969 in Budapest, where it was agreed to form a permanent defense council composed of the defense ministers of the member countries. The powers and responsibilities of this new council have not yet been clearly defined, particularly as they might affect those of the Soviet-dominated High Command structure of the Warsaw Treaty. But, at any rate, this new body seems a far cry from the suprastate authority Moscow would evidently like.

Second, it wants a reorganization of COMECON involving closer integration of the planning processes of the member states and greater coordination of the use of their resources and their foreign trade policies. This, in principle, is a return to Khrushchev's proposals for a suprastate planning authority abandoned in 1964 mainly, but not solely, because of Rumanian recalcitrance. The Soviet proposals, however, are not known in detail and it seems they would settle for something less than Khrushchev's plan, presumably because of continuing Rumanian opposition, the hesitation of other states like Hungary and Czechoslovakia, and the sheer technical difficulties attendant on establishing and operating such a body. The session of COMECON held in East Berlin in

January 1969 seemed to have agreed on little except to study the matter further, indicating the numerous difficulties involved.

Third, it wanted the World Conference of Communist Parties, which was held in June 1969, to establish a new political-ideological framework defining—if not in so many words—Soviet hegemony not only in Eastern Europe but also in that part of the world communist movement represented at the Moscow conference. Soviet motives in pressing for the conference were not solely predicated on their aims in Eastern Europe. The objective was to "legitimize" both their aims and the means of obtaining them.

On this score, the Soviets were only partly successful. They did obtain a compromise formulation of the duty of parties towards the international movement, as opposed to their own working class. Concessions were obtained, however, under circumstances that greatly reduced their political value to the Soviet leadership.

XV.

The Results of Soviet Efforts

Any assessment of the impact of the Czechoslovakia invasion on Eastern European-Soviet relations and of the degree of success of the Soviet efforts described above is inevitably influenced by a number of subjective considerations. Any valid assessment depends much on one's own estimate of these relations *before* the invasion and of the restraints that may be affecting Soviet intentions toward Eastern Europe *since* the invasion.

It is assumed that, on the eve of the invasion, the situation in Czechoslovakia was symptomatic—albeit in an extreme sense—of the centrifugal trends throughout Eastern Europe. These trends, affecting internal developments and external politics, had been in process since 1953 and were causing the most profound concern to the Soviet leadership. Any Soviet leadership would have been concerned by this situation, even one bent on reform at home and aware of the need for restructuring the alliance system. For the kind of leadership represented by Brezhnev, the concern proved intolerable. Czechoslovakia was by no means representative of the whole region, but the situation there epitomized the erosion of the Soviet position in Eastern Europe over the previous decade-and-a-half. Therefore, the invasion was not solely designed to discipline Czechoslovakia. It was also aimed to intimidate Rumania (and even Yugoslavia), and also those elements in the quiescent states (including the U.S.S.R. itself) receptive to the Czechoslovak inspiration.

Once the invasion had taken place, questions of where the Soviet Union went from there, and by what route, became the subject of considerable speculation. The dominant Soviet aims that became evident amounted to an impressive political-institutional effort to put Soviet hegemony in the region on a lasting foothold. But these aims do not add up to the Stalinist concept of hegemony that operated in Eastern Europe from 1948 to 1953. Even the more reactionary Soviet leaders of the present realize that the footing must not only be firm and lasting but also have some prospect of viability. And viability still demands the retention, albeit controlled and in a tighter framework, of some features of the autonomy the Eastern European states have acquired since 1953.

The existence of these restraints may give considerable leeway to any Eastern European state that wishes to take advantage of it. Within the confines of a Soviet-oriented foreign policy (including relations within the communist movement) and a domestic policy predicated on the active supremacy of the communist party, an Eastern European regime may still retain some freedom of maneuver. If such a regime is trusted by Moscow, it may, in that atmosphere of trust and in the context of agreement in principle on any policy to be adopted, be allowed to disagree with the Soviets on the implementation or even the feasibility of certain aspects of policy. Thus one may conjecture that it has only been intransigent Rumanians who have impeded progress toward a restructured Warsaw Pact and COMECON. Other states of more proven loyalty, professing general concurrence with Soviet aims, may have questioned specific Soviet proposals on the grounds of practicability and raised doubts as to their operational efficiency. It seems, as stated earlier, that in the very difficult problem of restructuring COMECON, Hungary and even occupied Czechoslovakia may have raised objections that, taken with Rumania's utter rejection of the whole idea, served to emasculate or shelve the Soviet proposal. And behind these objections or counter-proposals by a loyal ally like Kadar may well lurk the continuing factor of national self-interest, seeking to work within the Soviet dominated system rather than outside or against it.

In the pursuit of such self-interest, the Eastern European states (and not only Rumania) have continued to press for the maintenance and even increase of economic relations with the industrial west. East-west contacts of all kinds dipped sharply after the August invasions—largely due to cancellations or restrictions on the western side—but picked up again in 1969, particularly in the trade sector. It can be argued, of course, that such trade is thoroughly consistent with Soviet ambitions and is, therefore, actually encouraged by Moscow. But the political-economic implication of this trade, involving not only a western foothold in the Eastern European economy but also its impact on the rapidly rising technocratic classes of the region, can hardly be reassuring to the Soviet Union, especially when it is seeking to restructure its own trade bloc. The continuing rise in Bulgarian trade with West Germany, for example, and the successful application of Hungary for a Eurodollar loan for its aluminum industry do not easily fit the picture of a drastic reversion of Eastern Europe to its old satellite status. Rather, they suggest a framework that, though Soviet imposed, still allows for and is able to contain minor disagreements—even tensions—within the alliance.

Still it must be stressed again that the Czechoslovakia invasion and the Brezhnev doctrine of limited sovereignty may seriously inhibit Eastern European maneuvering within the framework. The Bonn Government's policy of building bridges to the East (Ostpolitik) to which several eastern bloc governments were at first receptive, became virtually a dead letter for some time because of Moscow's pressure on its allies. The Kiesinger-Brandt policy, an elaboration and acceleration of the policy begun by Erhard and Schroeder, sought to normalize relations with the Eastern European states both as an end in itself and, at least in the Erhard period, as a means of isolating the German Democratic Republic. The flaw in this policy was that it was predicated on the assumption that the Soviet Union would not, or could not, do anything to block a policy that then was viewed as a long-term threat to its own interests in this area of historic Russian-German rivalry. In what now seems an excessive indulgence in naïveté, the West German government seemed to have hoped that it could allay Soviet apprehensions on this score by keeping the Kremlin informed on the specific steps it intended to take. When Brandt became Chancellor the atmosphere seemed to change, at least permitting bilateral discussions to test the new regime. In this tactical shift, the Kremlin probed to explore new prospects for movement towards such goals as Bonn's diplomatic recognition of East Germany and of the present boundaries with Poland, and the political decoupling of West Berlin from the Federal Republic. The Soviets also hoped to gain support for calling a European security conference that would further the weakening of NATO and ultimately lead to a U.S. withdrawal.

As early as February 1967, immediately after the Rumanian decision to establish diplomatic relations with Bonn, the Soviet government, prodded by an alarmed Ulbricht and Gomulka, made it clear that it was against any other ally's doing the same. This ended the speculation that Hungary, Bulgaria, and Novotny's Czechoslovakia might soon follow Rumania's example. But Bonn persisted, with the emphasis now not so much on formal diplomatic links but on the improvement of economic, cultural, and political relations. This was done partly through the already established West German trade missions in Eastern European capitals, which, as time went on, could have assumed the de facto status of diplomatic missions. At the end of 1967, however, West German efforts scored a notable success with the agreement to resume diplomatic relations with Yugoslavia, and shortly afterwards the change of regime in Czechoslovakia raised new hopes that Prague would become the second Warsaw Pact (the third if Moscow is included) to exchange ambassadors with Bonn.

The invasion of Czechoslovakia ended these hopes and called for a complete reassessment of the premises on which the *Ostpolitik* had been based. Thereafter, Bonn's efforts (and those of the United States, for that matter) for a rapprochement with Eastern Europe would have to continue the roundabout route through Moscow. Of this, the Eastern European regimes were also very well aware. Moreover the Brezhnev doctrine, though not explicitly forbidding contacts of various kinds with Bonn, implicitly arrogated to Moscow the right of deciding when such contacts posed a danger to the socialist movement. It is this psychological inhibition that could be very important. This would mean a reversion to the condition of Eastern European-Soviet relations under Stalin. Hence, though there may still exist considerable leeway for the Eastern

European states in the new situation, skill will be needed to take advantage of it. It can be argued, of course, that such speculation rests only on an alarmist interpretation of the Brezhnev doctrine. Nevertheless, in view of the Soviet action against Czechoslovakia, it would be a bold or complacent Eastern European regime that based its policy on a more permissive view of that document.

XVI.

Some Specific Cases

The previous analysis has sought to give a general setting for discussions and predictions on the present and future course of Eastern European-Soviet relations. To fill out these generalizations and pinpoint exceptions, it is necessary to review briefly the range of possibilities as they might affect each country:

Czechoslovakia: The evident hesitation and indecisiveness of Soviet policy in post-invasion Czechoslovakia led to considerable optimism on the part of some analysts (and apparently of many Czechs themselves) that large and essential segments of the pre-August policy could be retained in the new situation. There was the passive resistance of the Czechoslovak people, bolstered by the quite new alliance among trade unions, intellectuals, and students, plus the continued defiance of some party leaders. These phenomena certainly seemed to present the Soviet Union with difficulties it was ill-equipped to handle. It hesitated to use force to crush resistance and terrorize the population, allowing its authority to be ostentatiously flouted. With the invasion over, moderation appeared uppermost in the shifting sands of Kremlin politics. This moderation was perhaps brought on by the need to mend as many international fences as possible and by uncertainty over the temper of the new Nixon Administration in Washington.

But, in the event, Soviet restraint and patience seem to have paid off, as the accession to party leadership of Gustav Husak in April 1969 indicates. Kremlin moderates in the post-August phase may all along have argued that such a development was inevitable in the end. After all, by the October 1968 treaty between the two states, Czechoslovakia was literally bound to the Soviet Union by hoops of steel. Subsequently, time and constant

Soviet pressure would produce a demoralization in the progressive ranks of the party and a creeping resignation among the people. This is what happened. True, the incident that brought the end of Dubcek was a high-spirited anti-Soviet riot prompted by a Czechoslovak defeat of the Soviet Union on the ice hockey rink. But the real state of Czechoslovak morale was shown by the people's resignation over the deposition of Dubcek and by the collapse of the pre-August front in the party, which crumbled rather than resist Husak. Soviet political policy in Czechoslovakia should not only be judged by its ineptitude in the second half of 1968 but also by its success in April 1969.

To try to predict the future course of Husak's policy is not easy. His domestic policy will be referred to more fully later; in foreign policy the question is, How far, within the tight limits any Czechoslovak leader must operate for the foreseeable future, will Husak act in the Czechoslovak national interest? His first task—and he has stated this unequivocally—has been to restore complete Soviet confidence in the Czechoslovak regime, something obviously lacking since the days of Novotny. To achieve this he adopted a foreign policy (some COMECON problems excluded) similar to that, for example, of Todor Zhivkov's regime in Bulgaria. Zhivkov virtually accepts the complete Soviet viewpoint. Similarly, in domestic policy he has been orthodox enough to allay any remaining Soviet fears about counter-revolutionary symptoms. Later, however, once confidence is achieved, it is by no means inconceivable that Husak will use whatever flexibility is available to him to pursue what he considers to be Czechoslovak interests. There are limits to the extent he can be cast as a Soviet puppet. He is in a situation where he must try to dispell national—particularly Czech—prejudice against himself. Indeed, though installed by Soviet pressure, his relationship with Moscow may become even less unequal than at first appeared. Because the Soviets have installed him, thus extricating themselves from a difficult situation, they have a vested interest in his success. This is particularly true, since he is heir of the first Soviet-engineered change in the Eastern European leadership since Brezhnev and Kosygin took power. And it is precisely this Soviet interest that gives Husak a certain bargaining power, if he cares to use it. In this sense there is a strong parallel between his position vis-à-vis Khrushchev. Khrushchev had a very strong interest in Kadar's survival and success. Kadar was not only installed by him in 1956, but later Kadar's domestic policy became a test case for the success of the type of reform-communism Khrushchev was seeking to promote both at home and abroad. There may be controversy on how far Kadar used the bargaining power available to him, but there is general agreement that it was there. Husak now finds himself in a similar position. His personality, which is stronger than Kadar's, may lead him to be more assertive.

Rumania: One of the most important by-products the Soviet leaders looked for from their invasion of Czechoslovakia was the bending of Rumania to a more obedient posture. It is precisely here, however, where the Soviet "intimidation credibility" seems so far to have been conspicuously ineffective. The Ceausescu regime, which had all along upheld the right of Czechoslovakia to choose its own domestic and foreign policy, refused to be cowed by the invasion. It took urgent steps in late August and early September to meet the possible threat of Soviet invasion. It has constantly repudiated the Brezhnev doctrine of limited sovereignty, defended its earlier decision to establish diplomatic relations with Bonn, and defiantly continued its rejection of any Soviet efforts to strengthen the eastern alliance, economically, politically, or militarily. It is true that it ceased its open condemnation of the Soviet action against Czechoslovakia soon after the invasion, probably because of Soviet warnings, but even on this most sensitive issue it resumed its open attacks at the Italian party congress in February.

There may be two explanations for Rumania's defiance and one does not necessarily exclude the other. The first is that, with all traditional Rumanian shrewdness and nerve, Ceausescu is gambling on the restraints affecting Soviet policy to save his country and his regime from the fate of Czechoslovakia. The second is that Ceausescu realizes that, though the danger of immediate invasion may have passed, Rumania is still in a state of siege and salvation is best assured by firmness rather than concessions. This would be both bold and wise. Any concessions of principle to the Soviet Union in this situation could be disastrous. They would demoralize the population, which had rallied around Ceausescu when the danger seemed immediate, and could have serious affects on party unity. Once a decision to make major concessions had been reached, there would inevitably be dissension on how much to concede. This, in turn, would not only damage Ceausescu's "legitimacy" in the eyes of both party and people; it would also create divisions within the party that Moscow would be quick to exploit. Thus, this second explanation for Rumanian conduct would complement rather than negate the first. Firmness and preparedness would provide the essential, additional security in case Bucharest's estimates of the restraints on Soviet action proved wrong.

Yugoslavia: Rumania's only Eastern European ally in the present situation is Tito's Yugoslavia. Both these states had looked with sympathy and hope on the pre-August developments in Czechoslovakia. They were anxious to add a third member to Eastern Europe's "club of independents" and recreate a Little Entente, this time directed against Soviet domination. The invasion not only dashed these hopes but also put Yugoslav security, as well as Rumanian, in some apparent jeopardy. By the measure committed, the Brezhnev doctrine could be taken as even more threatening to Yugoslavia than to Rumania. Ceausescu's reformist but conservative domestic policy can hardly be considered a threat to socialism by any but the most reactionary Soviet *apparatchik*. In contrast, both Tito's domestic and foreign policy are imbued with precisely those "counter-revolutionary" tendencies that are anathema to the Kremlin. But the immediate danger to Yugoslavia was clearly less than to Rumania. It is not a member of the Warsaw Pact, hence could not justifiably be held to fall within the purview of any sanctions the Soviet-dominated alliance might apply. Unlike Rumania, it has no common border with the Soviet Union and is, in general, a much more difficult country to invade and occupy successfully.

Even so, Yugoslavia's defiance of the Soviet Union since August has been remarkable both for its intensity and its bitterness. Not only has the Soviet action in Czechoslovakia been violently denounced but also the retrograde tendencies in Soviet domestic policy have been ruthlessly exposed. This was a luxury the Rumanians could hardly afford. On the other hand, Rumanian defiance in opposing Soviet demands for closer economic, political and military integration has been the more dangerous since it has been made from within an alliance Moscow is seeking urgently to strengthen for its own purposes. Yugoslavia, outside the alliance and thus less obliged to demonstrate active opposition, could become the spokesman, not only for itself, but also for those elements everywhere in Eastern Europe who stand for fundamental change in domestic and foreign policy. The reasons for the Yugoslav defiance were probably the same as those for the Rumanian: a shrewd assessment of the restrictions on Moscow's ability to act plus the decision that to concede would be more costly than to hold firm. In addition, Tito must also have been aware that any policy smacking of surrender would finally destroy his already tattered image as the world champion of non-alignment.

Ironically, the fear of Soviet action served to unite the Yugoslav nationalities more closely than they had been for many years. The fear may have been played up by the Yugoslav leaders precisely to check those centrifugal forces threatening to undermine the Federation. How long this unity can be maintained may depend a great deal on Soviet policy. If Soviet pressure or hostility is continued, then it will serve as an invaluable aid to Tito who, in the last years of his life, is seeking desperately to find solutions that could ensure Yugoslav stability and cohesion after his retirement or death. Patience, therefore, a traditional instrument of Csarist and Soviet foreign policy, may well dictate a less threatening posture toward Yugoslavia, thus hindering rather than helping the eleventh-hour effort to secure the state. For if Tito dies without the national question being solved or at least mitigated, serious factionalism is bound to result on political economic, cultural, and ethnic lines. Such factionalism would greatly increase the prospect of a powerful revival of Soviet influence, especially in the three republics of Serbia, Bosnia-Herzegovina, and Montenegro.

Albania: There is practically no solid evidence on which to

base meaningful analysis or speculation concerning Albanian relations with the Soviet Union. Three facts are, however, worth noting. The first is that in September Albania announced she was severing all formal connections with the Warsaw Pact organization. The second is that since the Soviet invasion of Czechoslovakia, Albania has made several gestures toward Yugoslavia, which, in the usual context of Albanian-Yugoslav relations, can be considered conciliatory. The third is that there was no Albanian delegation at the 1969 Chinese party congress.

The first two facts are mutually consistent. The formal withdrawal from the Warsaw Pact was motivated by the Soviet action against Czechoslovakia. It might be considered as a cautionary exercise in legalism aimed at removing any juridical justification Moscow may ever have wanted to use if it moved against Albania. (Although the point is hardly worth pursuing, it could be countered that, had the Soviets been so inclined, they could have used Albania's formal withdrawal from the Pact as precisely the justification they needed for action against her as it was in the case of Hungary in 1956). The conciliatory gestures toward Yugoslavia were also prompted by the Soviet move against Czechoslovakia. Albania, like China, denounced the Soviet invasion as heartily as the Yugoslavs, but from rather a different standpoint. These gestures, therefore, along with rumored Chinese attempts to improve relations with Belgrade, might be part of a Peking-inspired effort to explore every anti-Soviet avenue possible. It seems doubtful whether the exploration of this particular avenue will prove fruitful.

Obviously, the third fact, if it has any significance at all, is not consistent with the first two. The Albanian absence from the Peking congress may simply have been due to a Chinese wish not to wash their dirty linen in front of any outsiders. There were, after all, no delegations present from any foreign country. But this fact in itself may have been construed in Tirana as chilling reaffirmation of the Chinese policy trend, since the beginning of the Cultural Revolution, to concentrate almost entirely on domestic policy to the exclusion of foreign or allied interests. This, together with occasional reports of Albanian dissatisfaction with the extent and type of Chinese aid for their industry, now emerging from the purely extractive stage of development, might be prompting some members of the Albanian regime to reappraise their whole alliance with China. Certainly, the Soviet Union is aware of this possibility. Moscow has never written off Tirana entirely. Though Soviet trade with Albania ceased completely after the break, some Eastern European trade was allowed to continue. This can best be explained by a Soviet wish not to drive Albania into the arms of the west, as partially happened to Yugoslavia after 1948. An Albania tied to the west, notably Italy, would be harder to pry loose than an Albania tied to distant China. If, therefore, the Soviet Union decided that it was more in its interest to harass Yugoslavia than to let developments there take their own unhindered course, it might well put out feelers to Tirana suggesting massive economic aid and strong sympathy for Albanian irredentist claims to the Yugoslav Kosmet, where nationalism among the Albanian community has recently been causing much concern. Soviet military interest in reacquiring and reservicing the Sasseno submarine base might also be an added incentive in the new era of Russian naval presence in the Mediterranean.

Success for any such Soviet probing might have to be reached literally over Enver Hoxha's dead body, as well as those of several of his close associates. There is nothing to suggest insurrection in the Albanian party at the moment. Although the iron unity that has prevailed within the party for several years should not be viewed as permanent, even Hoxha himself might still carry out the needed about-face without falling. As for the Soviets, the new leadership could represent such a pro-Soviet turn as a triumph of common sense in making good the error of a blundering Khrushchev.

The German Democratic Republic: The salient question for some two years or more in the G.D.R.'s relations with the Soviet Union is the extent to which the East German regime, particularly Walter Ulbricht himself, has influenced Moscow in intra-bloc and international politics. It may seem a strange question to ask at all. An artificial creation at its inception, ruled by Soviet puppets installed and maintained by Soviet power, populated by a segment of a nation arbitrarily divided from the rest of its kin, the G.D.R. seemed, almost by definition, set for the permanent role of satellite.

It played such a role, by and large, until the dismissal of Khrushchev. Although it was evident that Ulbricht was deeply suspicious of the Soviet leader's periodic lunges toward détente with the west, particularly in his feelers toward Bonn at the very end of his career, there was little to suggest he had any perceptible influence on Moscow. Similarly his deep fears over the effects of Khrushchev's reform communism in Eastern Europe had no deterrent effect on its development, except, of course, within his own state. For many years, Ulbricht seemed little more than a frustrated Enver Hoxha, without Hoxha's opportunity and perhaps also without his reckless courage.

But the building of the Berlin Wall in 1961 led to important changes in the G.D.R.'s character and posture. Its people, cut off from escape to the west, reluctantly settled down to making the best of their new condition. The regime, now more self-confident, set about creating privileged sections of society, which, the reasoning ran, would have a self-interest in the perpetuation of the East German state. As part of this process a new technical elite was created, well trained and well paid, and given both responsibility and power in the state economy. The economy, for its part, took such an impressive upward turn after 1963 that the expression East German "economic miracle" began to be heard. Although the regime continued its conservative policy of repression in political and cultural affairs, a marked reformist tendency was noted in economic affairs to meet the challenges of a modern industrial society. Just how far Ulbricht has succeeded in his prime task of creating a distinctive East German national consciousness, based on the new privileged classes, is open to question. Some analyses, claiming outstanding success and strong popular support both for the regime and Ulbricht personally, seem very dubious. But it does seem clear that, over the last half-decade, the G.D.R. has emerged as a much stronger state than ever seemed likely throughout the 1950s.

It was always possible that this increase in economic weight—

at home and throughout Eastern Europe—would lead to increased political confidence if the opportunity came. It came with the fall of Khrushchev and the ensuing period of groping and indecision on the part of the new Soviet leaders. This apparently spurred Ulbricht to greater assertiveness on intrabloc matters pertinent to G.D.R.'s interests. (There is a striking parallel here with the trend in West Germany, where there is a growing demand that the F.R.G. use its great economic power to political and national advantage in the councils of the NATO alliance). Even before the fall of Khrushchev, Ulbricht's ideas on specialization within COMECON evidently had a strong influence on Soviet policy. After Khrushchev, however, this influence extended to international politics. His vehement reaction to Bonn's *Ostpolitik* and the prospect of West Germany's establishing diplomatic relations with several Eastern European states (along with Gomulka's similarly motivated obstinacy) finally prompted an initially hesitant Moscow to block Bonn's drive in early 1967. Similarly in the whole Czechoslovakia crisis, Ulbricht left no doubt from the very beginning where he stood on Czechslovak domestic developments and on the prospects of a rapprochement between Prague and Bonn. He and Gomulka were the joint sponsors of a policy aimed at the creation of an iron triangle comprising the G.D.R., Poland, and Czechoslovakia against West Germany. Czechoslovakia, even under Novotny, had always been hesitant; under Dubcek it was strongly opposed. For various reasons, therefore, Ulbricht sought to reverse the whole pre-August trend in Czechoslovakia and viewed the invasion with obvious satisfaction.

Accepting, however, the fact of his power and influence and the fulfillment of his policy regarding Czechoslovakia, it still remains very doubtful whether Ulbricht's influence is decisive enough to deter the Kremlin from a course it wished to take or to prompt it to adopt one against its inclinations. Ulbricht's influence has been magnified because: a) he has shown resolution on issues vital to G.D.R. self-interest on which Moscow, not so immediately affected or so narrowly preoccupied, may at first have seemed ambivalent; b) on such issues his leadership has from the first been united, whereas the Soviet Politburo has not; and c) in the end a majority in the Soviet Politburo has adopted the course Ulbricht urged because it deemed it in the Soviet interest to do so.

There may be similar instances in the future when this process repeats itself and Ulbricht's influence may appear to become even more decisive. But the limits of his influence will be clearly demonstrated when the interests of Pankow and Moscow do not happen to coincide. Such instance was the recent divergence in Soviet and East German attitudes toward the West German Communist Party.

Poland: If there is a sick man of Eastern Europe, then it must surely be Gomulka's Poland. The contrast between the exuberant hope of 1956 and the present bitter malaise represents a process of disintegration which, for speed and comprehensiveness, is unequalled anywhere in the whole of Europe. The Polish democratic situation is beyond the scope of this study; its deterioration, however, has caused an important shift of emphasis, if not a change of policy, in foreign affairs. Right up to the fall of Khrushchev, Poland retained some limited initiative in intrabloc and international affairs. It sought to restrain Khrushchev from his headlong collision course with the Chinese. For several years it was the most active Eastern European diplomatic scene and preserved at least tolerable relations with the United States. Now, though still preserving its internal autonomy, it has become one of the most vociferous proponents of bloc unity behind Moscow. To this the domestic debacle has decisively contributed. Indeed, in 1968, such were Gomulka's political difficulties within his own regime that, but for strong Soviet support, he might have been forced to surrender some of his power. But other factors have also contributed. Gomulka's own loss of energy and initiative; His distrust of the new trends in the communist world that cause disruption both domestically and internationally; The growing power of West Germany and his genuine, if exaggerated, fear of that power, particularly as it may affect the future of the Oder-Neisse frontier; His evident conversion to the notion that Poland's inadequacies in capital and raw materials can only be overcome by closer economic integration with the Soviet Union; The presence inside Poland of a powerful and resilient Roman

Catholic Church, which remains the living symbol of the strong westward orientation of the Polish heritage. So long as there is no change in leadership, there seems little possibility of its becoming anything other than the Kremlin's staunchist ally. Even if there were a change of leadership, with power falling into the hands of a more independent-minded group, it is highly doubtful whether the Soviet Union, provided it remained free to act, would tolerate Poland's becoming another Rumania. If one important reason for the invasion of Czechoslovakia was the fear for the Soviet position in Central Europe, such a consideration must apply even more strongly to Poland, the tragic victim of geopolitics throughout modern history.

Hungary: In its relations with the Soviet Union since 1956 Hungary has made itself the victim of the "dilemma of one alternative." When the Soviet Union is in a position where a radical choice seems necessary, then Kadar can only move with Moscow. This was the case with the Sino-Soviet dispute and with Czechoslovakia. Before the threshold of a radical choice on the Soviets' part is reached, however, Kadar has been able to play a role of some autonomy and even independence. Like Gomulka, he sought to restrain Khrushchev in the Sino-Soviet dispute and his efforts at mediation between Prague and Moscow in 1968 are well-known. His self-appointed role is always that of a moderator, seeking to avoid rifts and clashes, trying to preserve an atmosphere of calm in which he can proceed with his domestic reforms and perhaps also quietly push his schemes of Danubian cooperation, his only foreign policy initiative so far.

The more moderate Soviet leaders probably welcome Kadar's role in bloc politics. It is occasionally a useful propaganda play for Moscow. He is at once a demonstration of the "independence and sovereignty" of all communist regimes and parties, and, in the final analysis, an exemplar of Kremlin-ruled, true "proletarian internationalism." It is doubtful, however, whether this appreciation is shared by the more intractable, less subtle members of the Soviet hierarchy. Opinion on Kadar in the Moscow leadership may well be divided and the doubts about him may extend to his policy at home—liberal by current Soviet standards—as well as abroad. Thus, if Soviet policy continues its conservative course, Hungarian-Soviet relations may become considerably worse unless Kadar retreats into the role of unquestioning puppet.

Bulgaria: In a sense, the difference between Hungary's relations with the Soviet Union, and those of Bulgaria are large enough quantitatively to involve a difference in quality. The Zhivkov regime sides with Moscow long before the threshhold of radical choice is reached. There is, in fact, little evidence to suggest that Bulgaria has ever opposed Soviet policy. In the late 1950s, however, it did show a certain fascination with Chinese domestic policies and, in the early 1960s, it may well have made clear to Khrushchev that it wished to proceed with its full-scale industrialization program despite demands by the G.D.R. and Czechoslovakia that it specialize mainly in agricultural products and raw materials. The fact that Bulgaria was allowed to proceed with its program while Rumania only got its way after a disruptive dispute has never been adequately accounted for. If the reason lay in Moscow's confidence in Bulgaria's political and international loyalty, and its lack in Rumania's case, then this would indeed be a spectacular illustration of what has been the main theme of Bulgarian-Soviet relations. Bulgaria's loyalty has brought very substantial economic rewards. Moscow has not simply bought Sofia's loyalty, of course. This would imply a deliberate choice between alternatives, crediting the Bulgarian regime with a flair and nerve it has never possessed. The weakness and mistakes of the Zhivkov regime and the traditional background of pro-Russian sentiment have also contributed to Bulgaria's strong adherence. But the interplay of loyalty and reward has been the main characteristic of relations between the two states.

It is likely to remain so. What could disturb it is the momentum that Bulgarian feeling on the Macedonian issue has acquired, taking the form of surrogate nationalism. As long as Moscow's policy of hostility toward Yugoslavia continues, then Sofia's campaign about the Bulgarian character of all Macedonians is tolerable, even useful for the Soviet Union. If this policy changed, however, the Bulgarian regime would be in a dilemma because it would be much harder for it to subdue the popular passions and expectations it has aroused. This could create difficulties between Sofia and Moscow and might even prompt some Bulgarian leaders to seek bargaining strength in the fact that their country is the Soviet Union's principal ally in the Balkans, with a most important strategic location adjoining the two unstable western allies, Greece and Turkey.

XVII.

Prospects in Eastern Europe

The essential characteristic of Czechoslovak internal development in the hectic months between January and August 1968 was that, despite official Prague statements, the traditional role of the communist party in society was indeed being modified. Party supremacy, as understood in its Leninist concept, was being replaced by party guidance. Within the party, democratic centralism was no longer the cardinal rule. Even after a majority decision had been taken, dissent from it would still be tolerated. In the society as a whole, the party was no longer to be considered the sole source of initiative and change. Other institutions and pressure groups could now originate proposals for change and reform. It was this accepted spontaneity that gave the Czechoslovak spring its refreshing and stimulating character.

But it was anathema to the Soviet leadership and the fear of its consequences was probably the most important single reason for the decision to invade. By its action Moscow served notice that there was a definite limit beyond which internal reform should not proceed, and that the limit was any modification of the supremacy of the communist party.

This does not necessarily mean that the word reform itself is now banned or that Moscow is insisting on a course of reaction in Eastern Europe. Reform may proceed provided it is originated and directed by the party and does not endanger it. Economic reform, therefore, will presumably continue in Hungary and, in a modified form, in Czechoslovakia too. A controlled political and cultural relaxation, even the tolerance of embryonic pressure groups, does not specifically fall within the purview of the Brezhnev doctrine. The Soviet leaders may not like such developments, but they hardly seem in a position to reestablish the relationship of the late 1940s.

For this reason, the domestic policy of the Kadar regime takes on a new importance in Eastern Europe. The nature and scope of Kadar's reforms probably represent the maximum that can be envisaged without serious strain for the country concerned with Moscow. So long as Kadar maintains his reform policy he will remain an example and a yardstick for other Eastern European rulers so inclined. Yugoslavia, of course, has since August resumed its unique role as the revisionist example that will not be tolerated. But Yugoslavia will remain the spur and inspiration for all those non-ruling sections of Eastern European society, communist and non-communist, who seek radical, qualitative change. If it can stay united and stable, it will pose a serious threat to Soviet ideological and political supremacy in Eastern Europe simply because of the fascination its internal reforms will exert.

Party-controlled reform, even extensive reform, as in Hungary, is still therefore an option. There are, however, new factors in the situation that could impose obstacles to its implementation. First, the inhibitive shock of the Soviet invasion itself, designed to crush Czechoslovak reform, will take time to wear off. Before it does there may well be a tendency toward numbed immobility. Secondly, the invasion, an emanation of the apparatus revival in the Soviet Union, must have greatly encouraged the forces of apparatus conservatism within the Eastern European Parties. It will be more difficult for the reformist elements in these parties to gain acceptance for their policies. Finally, there are the inhibiting implications of the Brezhnev doctrine. As has been said, this does not exclude reform but, as in the case of foreign policy, it could have the serious psychological impact of inducing Eastern European rulers to err on the side of caution. This caution might also be reflected in their following of Soviet patterns rather than initiating their own. Thus the Soviet Union could once again become the pace setter for internal change, a role it had lost by the end of the 1950s. Recent developments suggest that, if this is the case, the pace will be slow indeed.

From a longer-term perspective, of course, it can be argued that the invasion of Czechoslovakia and its shorter-term consequences represent only an interruption of the erosion of Soviet hegemony, a temporary check to those basic, irreversible trends in Eastern Europe that were gathering momentum before the invasion took place. These were: The revival of nationalism; Growing political economic and social pluralism; The erosion of communist ideology; The decline of communist party supremacy. All these trends, fundamentally detrimental to the Soviet position, could be checked, the argument might run, but not halted. Therefore, the Soviet Union has simply shored up a crumbling edifice, but the edifice is bound to fall in the long run, whatever the efforts to preserve it. Only a completely new edifice can accommodate the inexorable trends in motion throughout the whole region.

This argument is generally a sound one, but has become so familiar that it is hardly worth expounding. Moreover, until there are far-reaching changes in the Soviet Union resulting not only in new leaders but also in a new political ethos, there will be no attempt to build a new edifice. Shoring-up operations should continue to be the order of the day for some time to come. They may be violent or non-violent. The invasion of Czechoslovakia was one type; the June world communist conference another. The Brezhnev doctrine provides the crucial veil of legitimacy for the whole shoring-up operation. Thus while we continue to watch the irreversible trends, submerged and re-emerging, we must also analyze the power of these shoring-up operations to delay change. The Czechoslovakia invasion may have considerably delayed the process.

Looking to the next decade, the world can expect that the leadership crisis in the Soviet Union will be temporarily resolved and that a sudden massive generational shift will occur in Soviet leadership. This new leadership, unlike the existing one, will be largely a product of the post-Stalinist era. While it will not be crippled by the cruel Stalinist legacy, nor ideologically committed to the corpus of Stalinist mythology, it may prove no less difficult to deal with. Since the question of how this coming generation of Soviet leaders will interpret the Soviet past is unknown, it is extremely likely that our assumptions concerning Soviet behavior and purpose will continually be subject to critical re-examination and reassessment.

PART THREE

Individual Panelist Comments

European Panelists

Sir William Hayter I am in general agreement with this paper, but have some dissent on points of varying importance.

In regard to a power struggle in Soviet leadership leading to "deeds of an explosive nature" (p. 10) etc., I think this exaggerates the dangers. I do not myself see anything in the present internal Soviet situation that makes me think the present leaders likely to undertake dangerous foreign adventures. I also think the party apparatus as a power base should not be downgraded excessively. It seems to me to be at least as significant a power base as any of the others named, and more so than some, e.g., the bureaucratic apparatus.

I doubt that the Soviet fear of Bonapartism (p. 11) is really as significant a factor as is indicated. The only possible potential Bonaparte of recent years, Marshal Zhukov, was brushed off by Khrushchev without the slightest difficulty or worry.

In the section on state vs. ideological interests (p. 13 ff), it should not be implied that the Soviet leaders would like to distinguish between the two but cannot. Factors of traditional policy and ideology enter into all levels of policy formulation in the U.S.S.R.

I know of no evidence for the statement that the Soviet government would resist a unified *communist* Germany. It might well be inconvenient for them, but they could not possibly veto it.

I also do not believe that the chances of action against Rumania are as small as stated in the paper (p. 133).

Professor Alec Nove On matters less directly my specialist concern, I believe that the panel overstresses the political nature of technical arguments in top-level Soviet decision-making (p. 10). Under Stalin, people were shot and imprisoned for being on the losing side of such technical matters as crop rotations, or cruisers versus submarines. One of of the big changes surely is that this is no longer always or even often so. As in any country, advocacy of a point of view affects the promotion prospects of the advocate.

I entirely agree with what the panel says about chauvinism (p. 10), except that I see no sign of an escalation of competitive chauvinism. Who is competing with whom in aggressive postures? I see much more a picture of negative security-mindedness.

The panel asserts rather dogmatically that Brezhnev has a special relation with the military (p. 11). Is this so? It also asserts that "the person who forfeits army support loses." Suppose the sentence read: "The person who loses forfeits army support." That too would be consistent with the evidence!

In regard to negotiations with the Soviets (p. 15 ff), I do not think that anyone on the panel conceived of a change in the "basic mentality" of the Russians. There may, however, be a gradual whittling away of certain ideological commitments, or rather their relegation to a lower position on the list of priorities. In this connection, one must surely mention China, since a gigantic and hostile neighbour led by a communist party cannot help but affect the outlook of the leaders both on communism and on the world, whatever their basic mentality may be.

Dr. Gebhardt von Walther I have the impression that reform of the Soviet economy, especially industry, is just as important and decisive now as ever. Current economic problems are, however, much more difficult to solve, given that industrialization has become much more diversified, complicated, and much more difficult to handle from one center. For example, the lack of appropriate computers cannot be overcome. Industrialization in the Soviet Union is an ideological problem and thus is directly related to the social structure. Therefore certain problems that seem to us purely economic become more complex for being linked with ideology.

If you underline, and rightly, the difficulties in agriculture (p. 8), you must not forget the great organizational difficulties in the domain of services and distribution (*Dienstleistungsbetriebe*). Even the Russians agree that in their system individual initiative, so efficient in capitalism, can never be reached.

I am of the opinion that the word "Stalinism" is used in too many ways. Restalinization is over-advertized outside the Soviet Union. That the governmental system or that the methods of ruling the country have hardened and will be hardened even more does not imply restalinization in the Western sense. Ruling *c kulakom* in this gigantic country, with so many different nationalities and such inclination for individualism, has a different meaning from that which the same practice would have in Western countries.

I am personally of the opinion that the influence of the armed forces (p. 10), outside of purely technical questions of military policy, will always be insignificant, whereas the influence of the party apparatus will always be predominant. The apparatus can develop into a mighty instrument in the hands of an ambitious party man.

The interpretation of the notion "coexistence" has changed only once: in the time of Khrushchev after the Cuban crisis. The newest definition, as far as I know, is the one given by Andropov on the occasion of the 50th anniversary of the K.G.B. and I think it is still valid.

In regard to what policies are required of the states of Eastern Europe (p. 16 ff), one might suggest: primacy of the party, predominance of the Politburo, absolute exclusion of freedom of the press, of assembly, and of speech. These are, amongst others, the absolute limits which cannot be trespassed.

Dr. Gerhard Wettig On the whole, I feel it is a rather well-balanced summary, to which I would not hesitate to subscribe as far as I feel myself competent. But, I would offer a dissenting vote.

Soviet military intervention in Czechoslovakia, in my view, shows increasing sensitivity to nonconformist trends within the Soviet power sphere, even though such trends are still communist and pro-Soviet in their self-perception. It shows a decreasing sense of risks involved in forceful actions that do not touch NATO states directly. Soviet politicians and Soviet mass media have made abundantly clear that any Eastern European development that does not remain within the limits prescribed by Moscow and that goes out of Soviet control is regarded as a threat to socialism as defined by the Kremlin. Moreover, it is the active détente policies of some Western countries, notably the Federal Republic of Germany, that are made largely responsible for a decrease of Soviet discipline in Eastern Europe. This would have been unthinkable during the cold war period. Western détente, as far as it does not favor Soviet goals like elimination of U.S. power from Europe (as in the case of Johnson's Non-Proliferation Treaty policies), is perceived as dangerous to Soviet power and to Moscow-oriented Communist orthodoxy. It involves the risk of increased contact and communication between east and west and within the Soviet orbit. Hence, the movement of the Czechoslovakian reformers is described as "indirect" or "social aggression" and as "veiled" or "subversive attacks" from the "imperialistic world" against the socialist community.

Soviet comments have explained that, in consequence of the experiences in Czechoslovakia, the principle of peaceful coexistence must be applied in a much more restricted sense than before. It has to be accorded validity only insofar as it favors the Soviet cause against the west, but not vice versa. Soviet military action in Czechoslovakia has destroyed European hopes that there might be a détente in the course of which the east-west tensions might be gradually softened and perhaps even in the long run overcome.

American Panelists

Abraham Brumberg

In recent years it has become fashionable to employ sundry permutations of the word "Stalinism" to describe events in the Soviet Union since March 1953. "Destalinization" having (for understandable reasons) fallen into disuse, we now hear a good deal about "restalinization," "quasi-stalinism," or "neostalinism." While the last two of these terms strike me as more apposite to the current situation than the first, I would nevertheless suggest that the time has come to abandon these semantic efforts altogether.

The reason for this modest proposal is that the Soviet political system—as distinguished from Soviet *society*—remains basically the same as the one constructed by Stalin. The political terror of 1935-38, much as the brutal industrialization and collectivization drives that preceded it, were not the essential operative characteristics of the Stalinist system. Rather, they represented its excesses or, more accurately, various stages in its march to consolidation. There seems to be little doubt that Stalin himself had come to believe in the necessity of his own brand of "permanent revolution," or what some observers have called the "revolution from above." That is, he had become addicted to the notion that nothing short of periodic "shake-ups" would assure the viability of his system, as well as the viability of his personal rule. The tightening of political controls after World War II, Zhadnov's "cultural purges" of the late 1940's, the subsequent "anti-cosmopolitan" campaign, and the indications of impending purges in 1952-53, culminating in the "Doctor's Plot" of January 1963, all testify to it. Yet none of these artificially induced crises was of the same magnitude as the bloody slaughters that paved the way to Stalin's absolute power and to the consolidation of the Stalinist system. More, they were "irrational"—that is, they were not determined by pragmatic considerations of ruthless "social engineering" (such as the slaughters of the land-owning peasantry and of Stalin's real and potential opponents), but rather by the personal predilections of an increasingly paranoid dictator. This was demonstrated by the fact that Stalin's successors clearly dissociated themselves from these policies even as his body was lying in state. The link between the purges of the 1920's and the 1930's and those of the last period of Stalin's rule—and thus one of the fundamental features of the Stalinist system—was the very *existence* of the instrument of terror. And that instrument, along with many other instruments and institutions endemic to Stalinism, has not been renounced by the new leaders; it remains with us to this day.

This is not to argue, of course, that there have been no significant changes in the Soviet Union in the past 17 years. The changes have been many as well as profound. They were initiated, as I have already indicated, immediately after Stalin's death, and they were greatly accelerated following Khrushchev's famous speech in February 1956. But it seems to me that we must make a distinction between the changes that have occurred within the political system, or body politic, and those within the society at large.

To be sure, the two are interrelated. The limited political reforms initiated by Khrushchev—in the first place, the abandonment of mass terror and the efforts to provide the Soviet citizen with at least a modicum of legal protection against arbitrary arrest and execution— have greatly altered the mentality and behavior of important segments of the Soviet population; and these changes, in turn, have made it progressively more difficult for the Soviet leaders to resort to some of the methods of their predecessor, much as they may have been tempted to do so on numerous occasions. The processes that were set in motion in 1953-56 can be partially arrested, and even partially reversed. The continuing repressions of Russia's dissidents is surely a case in point, contrasting, as it does, with some of the more permissive periods of Khrushchev's reign. Yet the existence and persistence of widespread dissent and protest in the U.S.S.R. illustrate the profound changes that have taken place in Soviet society. They also demonstrate the inability of the authorities to deal with these manifestations as effectively as Stalin, the continuing availability of the terror apparatus notwithstanding. To speak, therefore, of "restalinization," and to describe "the downfall of Khrushchev . . . as being nearly as important as the death of Stalin, [though] with opposite consequences" (p. 26) is, in my opinion, to misread the entire development of the Soviet Union since 1953, which is far more variegated and dynamic than the terms "Stalinism," "destalinization," "restalinization" or, for that matter, "neostalinism," would imply.

Soviet society today, then, is hardly the same as that of 20 or 30 years ago. The dismantling of the myths of an omniscient leader and of an infallible party, and the legitimization of criticism (however limited), have bred a spirit of skepticism, of inquiry and, finally, of outright defiance and opposition to the regime, all of which would have been totally unthinkable 20 years, or even 10 years ago. It is not merely "the intelligentsia who resist the cultural crackdown by passing underground manuscripts from reader to reader." Students and even workers have gone out on the streets protesting the Soviet invasion of Czechoslovakia. Violations of the constitutional right to religious freedom have been denounced by hundreds of Baptists, Evangelical Christians, and members of the Russian Orthodox Church. Thousands of Crimean Tartars have demonstrated against their continued exile and suppression of their national and cultural identity. Soviet Jews have openly renounced their citizenship and proclaimed their desire to go to Israel. Distinguished scientists have affirmed their belief in freedom of speech and in the values of political democracy. The overall number of active protesters and dissidents is not very large; nor, thus far at least, do the issues they've championed reflect the most important grievances of the Soviet population as a whole, which may well help to explain the reluctance of the regime to deal with dissent in a more decisive manner, its reliance on selective repression and, occasionally, on partial concessions.

In this respect, the policies of the Brezhnev-Kosygin regime are not markedly different from those of Khrushchev, even though the current emphasis is assuredly on repression, for which the image of Stalin serves as a useful political symbol. Khrushchev's ten-year tenure saw recurrent oscillations between repression and concessions, between coercion and incentives. While on balance his policies certainly resulted in a considerable liberalization of the Soviet system and society, the policies of his successors may yet bear similar results, if only because limited reprisals and the absence of any significant economic progress are likely to exacerbate the latent discontent of the Soviet population.

Whether the current period is one of "transition" (as argued by some of the panelists), or whether the pattern now followed by the Soviet leadership can go on "indefinitely" remains to be seen. The term "transition" implies an ineluctable progression to a qualifiedly

new stage of development; and it is by definition impossible to predict whether anything will or will not
endure "indefinitely." It is altogether likely that the
mounting internal and external pressures will indeed
force a radical change—perhaps another "palace coup,"
perhaps the rise of a military dictatorship, perhaps even
a series of sporadic revolts from below. It is equally
possible that the leadership will continue to maneuver
and muddle along its present ambivalent course for years
to come. There is also another alternative: that as a
result of vacillation on top and unrest below the regime
will embark upon a course of minor concessions that
will, in turn, pave the road for further relaxations and
reforms. It would be a brave man indeed who would
place his bet on any of the various alternatives of which
there are surely legion.

Dr. Richard I should like to draw the attention of the reader to
V. Burks three points.

The first of these concerns the concept of "restalinization." As presented (p. 26), this concept appears
to mean a reversion to the Stalinist system, which was,
in the last analysis, government by terror systematically
applied by the security police. The upgrading of the
secret police and the increase in the number of concentration camps is spoken of. There may be evidence for
such assertions, but if so it has escaped me. In any case
I would doubt that what we are witnessing in the Soviet
Union today is a return to the Stalinist system, for that
system has shown itself incompatible with the successful
management of an advanced industrial economy, a stage
of development that the Soviet Union has now reached.

Rather, it seems to me, we should conceive of
restalinization as an effort to prevent the totalitarian
system of controls from eroding away in circumstances
in which these controls cannot be reenforced by dosages
of terror. Sinyavsky and Daniel were imprisoned, not

so much because what they had written was critical of Soviet reality as because they had published in Western Europe without the permission of Soviet authority. Had they succeeded in this practice, they would have created a dangerous precedent, for whatever is published by Soviet authors in the West, especially if it is critical, has a tendency to return to the Soviet Union by way of Western radio broadcasts or in the valises of Soviet travellers. Sinyavsky and Daniel were punished as examples to make clear that the authorities in Moscow would not permit evasion of censorship by the device of publication abroad.

Similarly, Soviet emphasis during the Czechoslovak crisis on maintaining the leading role of the party was motivated, among other things, by Prague's abolition of censorship. The Soviet leaders had difficulty imagining how they could continue to impose censorship on the Soviet writers if the intelligentsia of a dependent country were freed from it. The military occupation of Czechoslovakia was in part intended to protect the institution of censorship in the world capital of socialism. Thus the phenomenon of restalinization should be seen as an effort to dam up forces of change in part released by the policy of destalinization, rather than as a reversion to Stalin's system itself.

The second point which I should like to address concerns the possibility of a Soviet military occupation of Rumania (p. 32). I am inclined to doubt that this eventuality would depend to any considerable extent upon the preoccupation of the great powers with conflict elsewhere. Exactly as in the case of Czechoslovakia, the Soviets will invade Rumania only as an act of desperation, when Soviet leaders feel that the vital interests of the Soviet state are at stake. The cost of invasion is very high. In the Czechoslovak case it has included public condemnation of the Soviet Union by virtually all the communist parties of the free world, and by many ruling parties as well; a basic change in the relations between the Czech and the Russian populations; and a state of affairs within the occupied country that can only be described as a shambles. In Rumania, the cost might be even higher, since the Rumanian leaders have publicly asserted on a number of occasions that, in the event, they would resist by force of arms.

The experience of Czechoslovakia is instructive. Moscow realized that the Czechoslovak Communist party, supported by the overwhelming majority of the Czech and Slovak peoples, was in process of dismantling the dictatorship of the proletariat and replacing it with a one-party social democracy. If this development were not prevented, the very existence of the East German and Polish regimes would be called in question (how could one deny the Poles what one permitted the Czechs?), and perhaps even the existence of the Soviet regime itself. In other words, the U.S.S.R. would almost certainly occupy Rumania if either a) the Rumanian party attempted to dismantle the Marxist-Leninist system and replace it with another or b) the Rumanian regime appeared to be losing control of the population, or were about to be overthrown. Neither of these eventualities seems very likely in the predictable future.

Concerning the question of the possible conflict between Soviet national interests and communist ideology (p. 26), it appears that there already exists at least one instance in which the two are directly in conflict, the instance of the quarrel with the Chinese. Had China not been conquered by the Communists, the clash with Peking . . . over boundaries, over the leading role in Asia, and so on . . . would have been both far less damaging and far less dangerous to the Soviet protagonist. The conflict would very probably not have involved a challenge to Soviet leadership of the world communist movement, nor the loss of Soviet control over the regimes in Albania and Rumania, nor yet the existence of Peking-oriented splinter parties throughout the world. The question of Soviet assistance to the Chinese nuclear weapons program would not even have arisen, while the problem of the extent of Soviet aid to China would have a entirely different aspect.

The conflict between Soviet national and Soviet ideological interests in the Chinese case gives rise to the possibility of a similar contradiction emerging in the relationship of the Soviet Union to Eastern Europe. Communist Moscow has lost control of the communist regimes in Yugoslavia (1948), Albania (1961) and Rumania (1963) and found her control of the Bulgarian regime threatened in 1965. Soviet troops suppressed a rising in East Germany in 1953 and had to be sent to Hungary in 1956 and to Czechoslovakia in 1968 to restore communist regimes in those countries; military intervention in Poland in 1956 was averted only at the eleventh hour. In a 20-year period each and every communist regime in Eastern Europe has either been threatened with violent overthrow or has turned against the Soviet patron.

When communism was imposed on Eastern Europe the area had much greater importance as a military glacis than it does now, under the conditions of nuclear stalemate. In 1945 the Soviets also thought of the areas as a substantial accretion to their military-industrial potential; hence the very rapid pace of industrialization and the exaggerated emphasis on heavy industry. The new East European industry would be fed with the inexhaustible raw material resources of the Moscovite center and would in exchange pour a stream of manufactured wares into the voracious Soviet market. But today, 20 years after the formulation of this policy, the industrial facilities of the East European countries appear to the Moscovites in the guise of an unnecessary and expensive duplication of their own heavy industry.

The quality of the manufactures delivered is distinctly second rate. The resources of the U.S.S.R. no longer seem inexhaustible, while it is now clear that they cannot be extracted at free world costs. The industrial technology that the Soviets need to compete with the West can, for the most part, still be bought only in the West. On the one hand, the Soviets have begun to charge the Eastern Europeans above-world-market prices for raw materials; on the other hand, they have permitted trade with Eastern Europe, taken as a percentage of total soviet trade, to remain stagnant or to decline.

Meantime Eastern Europe has come to function as an ideological trojan. The collapse of communism in an East European country calls into question the stability of the Soviet regime itself. Western capitalist subversionary techniques (interest rates, public opinion polls, freedom of the press) find a ready reception among East European communists, who camouflage them as socialist inventions and make them politically available to unstable elements within the Soviet Union itself. As a zone of transition, Eastern Europe has much greater impact on Russian than upon the countries of the Common Market, precisely because it is ruled by communists. At some point in the 1970s or 1980s will not the Soviet leaders be brought to consider whether these vital interests would not have been better served by an Eastern Europe arranged on the Finnish model?

Foy D. Kohler I should like to make clear that I am not one who takes the extremist view that restalinization is the most decisive development in the Soviet Union since 1964 (p. 26). There has certainly been a reversion to orthodoxy. The term "neostalinism" is certainly preferable, although even this I think tends to give a somewhat exaggerated impression of the significance of the very restrained and limited program to rehabilitate the image of Stalin.

With reference to the situation in Eastern Europe, I agree that the maintenance of the G.D.R. is a costly and somewhat difficult proposition but would not go so far as to call it a wasting asset (p. 29). On the contrary, I think Moscow regards the G.D.R. as a keystone in the Eastern European arch and that whatever the difficulties, the Kremlin leadership will hang on there indefinitely.

On foreign policy, I think the decisions are taken (by Soviet leaders) largely on a pragmatic basis, in the light of prevailing global circumstances. Even those in the Kremlin who participate in the decisions would have difficulty in sorting out the exact mix of ideology as against national interest motivation.

Finally, I think the term "peaceful co-existence" is used somewhat too loosely and without quotes in the summary paper. To me the Soviet definition of "peaceful co-existence" is almost precisely my definition of "Cold War." In this sense I think we are in for an antagonistic but cautious relationship between the United States and the Soviet Union for some time to come, whatever term one prefers to use to describe that relationship.

Wolfgang Leonhard The panel findings seem to assert (p. 27) that while Khrushchev indulged in deliberate falsification, distortion, and denunciation of Stalin, the post-Khrushchev leadership places the whole issue of Stalin in an historically more accurate perspective. My disagreement with this position stems from my belief that destalinization under Khrushchev was more than mere propaganda and personality attack, and that the current restalinization is more than just the revival of Stalin as an historical figure.

Although Khrushchev unquestionably used his attacks on Stalin propagandistically to serve political power interests, his criticisms were based on correct facts. If any fault may be found, it is that the criticisms failed to reveal the full nature of Stalin and of the Stalinist system. Instead of calling Khrushchev's accusations vilifying, one-sided presentations, falsifications, distortions, and denunciations, I would emphasize the positive role they played in disassociating the modern Soviet Union from the mass terrorism of the Stalin era. Khrushchev's attacks on Stalin laid the political, as well as the psychological foundation for the destalinization reforms in the Soviet Union.

I sharply disagree with the paper's position on the importance of restalinization (pp. 70 ff). I see restalinization as being much more ominous for future developments in the Soviet Union than the halt of the destalinization process or the revival of the memory of Stalin, the man. Restalinization is not just a kind of "correction of the picture" (p. 63 ff) necessitated by Khrushchev's supposed excesses, but rather the foundation for a harsher line.

In stating that destalinization continues (p. 68), the paper seriously underestimates the negative aspect of restalinization. The restalinization policy undermines all critical reforms and positive trends in Soviet society. It is a justification for a harsher line in cultural policy, authoritarian party discipline, the resurrection of the Secret Police, the opening of new camps, a harsher ideological line, and the rehabilitation of Stalinists who lost their positions during the Khrushchev period. I see the restalinization not only as a rehabilitation of Stalin as a person, but as an attempt to build a bridge to the Stalinist past—to silence any serious criticism of the entire Stalin era. I choose to call this policy of the post-Khrushchev leadership neostalinism.

Neostalinism does not mean a reduplication of Stalinism in the old sense, but rather the adaptation of Stalinist methods to new, changed conditions. Neo-stalinism differs from Stalinism in not emphasizing the club of personality (although this emphasis is increasing with Brezhnev); in placing less stress on heavy industry; and in replacing mass terror with increasing use of selective terror. I believe that the period of reform from above has ended under Khrushchev, and that the new leadership is trying to tighten the system as much as possible.

My next point concerns the nature of the Moscow-Peking conflict. The paper refers to "Mao's open bid for some 500,000 square miles of Soviet territory" (p. 85). This supposed Chinese demand is, in fact, merely the propaganda of the Soviet Union. The Chinese Communists have always said they do not want the return of these territories. The only thing they want, and I think they are quite right, is for the Soviet Union openly to disassociate itself from Tsarist imperialist annexations and criticize them as did Marx, Engels, and Lenin. Soviet agreement to such a public statement would be quite enough to induce the Chinese to settle the border conflict at the conference table.

I was a little taken aback that the paper named foreign policy and military considerations as the primary explanation for the invasion of Czechoslovakia (p. 115 ff). I am especially skeptical of the idea that West Germany could continue to pose a "threat to Soviet influence in the area" (p. 117). Such an idea seems to imply that continued domination of Eastern Europe by the Soviet Union is justified from the military point of view. I personally think that the Soviet Union was not afraid of NATO in 1968 and that security justifications were merely an excuse. The Soviet Union was never afraid of West Germany ideologically and still less militarily as a threat to Czechoslovakia. Warsaw Pact forces were not sent to defend Czechoslovakia's western frontiers, but were deployed around Czechoslovakian cities. In effect, the Soviet Union behaved like a typical occupation power.

What the Soviet Union feared most was the Czechoslovak popularity. The main and overriding reason for the invasion was the Soviet Union's fear that the socialist camp would contain a country under a red flag and the leadership of a communist party, with a free press, a real operating parliament, independent trade unions and worker's councils, free travel, freedom to read and discuss Western newspapers, free literature and culture and a rule of law that does not proscribe free discussion. The Soviet Union feared that Czechoslovakia would inspire reform forces in East Germany, Poland, Hungary, and the Soviet Union itself. I think that Soviet leaders later played up the so-called security considerations and the fear of West Germany in order to divert attention from the real reasons they were sending their troops into Czechoslovakia.

The idea that "Soviet restraint and patience seem to have paid off" (p. 131) for Soviet policy in Czechoslovakia after 1968 is misleading. Although the Soviet Union has not carried out mass terror in the manner of Stalin, the term "restraint and patience" is much too mild.

As far as long-term prospects for Eastern Europe are concerned, I wish to emphasize not just the revival of nationalism and autonomous forces (p. 146), but the reform tendencies crossing national boundaries. The struggle for political, economic, and social pluralism, the criticism of dogmatic Soviet ideology, and the insistence on a new model of socialism with a human face are the dimensions of a growing awareness in Eastern Europe of the importance of reform Communism.

Dr. Kurt L. London

Classical Marxism proclaimed that economics dominates politics. The development of events in the Soviet Union has shown that this has been reversed. I do not deny that Soviet economics may, under certain circumstances influence political considerations, but basically political decisions in the domestic and foreign fields are decisive. For that reason I do not believe that Moscow's economic position will directly affect the Soviet posture in the SALT talks (p. 26). Indirect influences may have some, but not necessarily decisive, effects on Soviet arms strategy. Furthermore, the demand by the army for increased resources will be either accepted or denied by the Politburo in accordance with prevailing views on the world situation. More than any other leadership, communist chieftains are political animals first and foremost. Since public opinion in communist-ruled countries is not nearly as influential as in the West and in some Third World countries, the members of the Politburo have a pretty free hand to interpret internal and external conditions and to make decisions according to their own lights, which have been and will inevitably be influenced by their long theoretical training and practical experience in a Marxism-Leninist state.

There is a contradiction when the panel states that ideology, as such, is declining as an instrument of political power (p. 26). Ideology is also pictured as having a very definite use. Furthermore, if you restrict this use to domestic politics, you have a Titoism of sorts. Communism still is being peddled in the outside world, although more cautiously. Restalinization equals reideologization, e.g., the doctrine of limited sovereignty which has a strong ideological motivation. I therefore suggest caution and would not shrug off the role of ideology in the determination of the Kremlin's policymaking. This is hard for Westerners to stomach, but it would be a serious mistake to denigrate the importance of Communist ideology and its impact on Soviet political behavior. The image of Stalin is being used by the present regime to bolster the new orthodoxy. It is interesting to note that the Stalinist *"Short History of the Communist Party"* has now been revised and put into circulation again. The isolated expressions of opposition to this orthodoxy, especially by some intellectuals, should not be overestimated. The Soviet leaders can and have suppressed them.

I am not in agreement with the panel's belief that the present pattern of Soviet domestic politics cannot go on indefinitely. It can indeed, at least for a very long time, and the presumed successors of the present Politburo are likely to be even tougher than the present incumbents. The fate of the Soviet Union is determined by its "ruling circles." There is no evidence these circles will veer away from basic Soviet tenets, even after the Soviet leaders have become more sophisticated in world affairs. They have refined their techniques to the extent where the Third World and Western policy makers have a hard time to put themselves into Soviet shoes. The party leadership can afford to direct the internal affairs of the U.S.S.R. as it sees fit.

Concerning the fascinating question as to whether ideology clashes with national interests (p. 26), I suggest that ever since the establishment of the Soviet state, there has been a dualistic attitude in Moscow's foreign policy: one arm pursuing national interests, the other, revolutionary aims. This has not necessarily cramped the style of Soviet politicians. The fact is that Soviet foreign policy consists of both communist and national elements which, during the years, have become amalgamated to such an extent that it is almost impossible to separate one from the other. It therefore follows that Soviet policies must be analyzed with the two elements in mind. In our interpretation of Soviet foreign policy, Moscow's dualism has not been sufficiently recognized. The western mind is too deeply affected by the concept of national interests as the main rationale of foreign policy.

Sino-Soviet relations (p. 33), of course, are important for the long-range development of world politics. In this connection no differentiation has been made between the Chinese position before and after the demise of Mao. With Mao gone, I believe that we can expect some changes that might be major and lead to an entirely different relationship not only between Moscow and Peking, but also, conceivably, between Peking and the outside world. This would pose new and extraordinarily difficult problems for American policy makers. While I admit that a post-Mao Sino-Soviet relationship might not be a very intimate one, even a working agreement between the two Communist powers would change the world political picture very considerably.

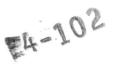